Somatic Therapy
for Children
with Autism

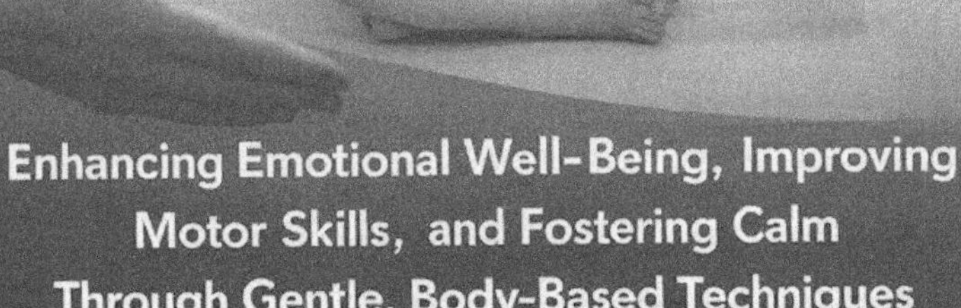

**Enhancing Emotional Well-Being, Improving
Motor Skills, and Fostering Calm
Through Gentle, Body-Based Techniques**

DR. HOPE ANDRUS

SOMATIC THERAPY

FOR CHILDREN WITH

AUTISM

A Guide to Enhancing Emotional Well-Being, Improving Motor Skills, and Fostering Calm Through Gentle, Body-Based Techniques

Dr. HOPE ANDRUS

Editorial Director:
Esther Matthew

Cover Design:
James Thomson

Editorial and Production Services:
True Pen Publishers

Copyright © Dr. Hope Andrus 2024.

All rights reserved.

Contents

Preface

Welcome to a journey of discovery, one that weaves together the power of somatic therapy with the unique needs of children on the autism spectrum. If you're here, chances are you're looking for answers, hoping to find tools that will help your child connect more deeply with their body, calm their mind, and feel more at peace in a world that often overwhelms them. You're in the right place. This book is designed to be your companion, offering not just insights and techniques, but encouragement and hope.

Somatic therapy is not just another therapy to add to the list—it's a gentle, body-based approach that can create profound shifts. It taps into the innate intelligence of the body, helping children with autism feel more grounded, less anxious, and better able to navigate the sensory challenges they encounter every day. For many parents, the idea of focusing on the body, rather than trying to change behavior or modify thinking, can be a revelation. It's an approach that recognizes that the body and mind are inextricably linked, and that when we help children tune into their physical sensations, we open a doorway to emotional regulation, improved motor skills, and even greater social ease.

One of the most exciting things about somatic therapy is that it doesn't require elaborate setups, expensive equipment, or rigid rules. It's accessible. Whether you're a parent, caregiver, or therapist, you'll find that the principles and practices in this book can be adapted to fit into the everyday rhythms of life. We'll explore simple, yet powerful exercises that can be done at home, at school, or in a therapeutic setting—movements that help children feel more connected to their bodies, calm their overstimulated nervous systems, and build resilience from the inside out.

Throughout this book, you'll also notice that the tone is not formal or clinical. That's intentional. This isn't just a manual or a guide—it's a conversation. As someone who deeply understands the challenges and joys of working with children on the spectrum, I want to speak to you in a way that feels personal, approachable, and supportive. Think of this as a friend or mentor walking alongside you, offering gentle guidance as you explore this new terrain. There will be ups and downs, moments of breakthrough, and times when you feel stuck. But together, we'll navigate these challenges with patience and compassion.

The truth is, no two children with autism are the same, and no two experiences of somatic therapy will be identical. That's part of the beauty of this work.

Somatic therapy is not about imposing a one-size-fits-all solution; it's about tuning into each child's unique rhythms, preferences, and needs. Some children may respond to certain exercises right away, while others will need time to warm up. It's a process—one that honors where your child is at right now and gently encourages them toward greater awareness, confidence, and calm.

In the following chapters, we'll explore the principles of somatic therapy in depth, breaking down how these body-based practices can help alleviate anxiety, reduce sensory overload, and improve motor coordination. We'll also look at ways to foster a supportive environment that helps your child thrive. But most importantly, we'll approach this journey with a spirit of curiosity and openness, recognizing that every small step forward is a victory worth celebrating.

As you read through the pages, I hope you'll find not just practical advice, but a sense of connection—a reminder that you're not alone in this. There's a growing community of parents, caregivers, and therapists who are discovering the benefits of somatic therapy for children with autism, and you're now part of that movement. Whether you're just starting out or have been exploring this path for some time, this book is here to support you, offering tools that can make a real difference in your child's life and, by extension, your own.

Together, we'll explore what it means to help children with autism feel more at home in their bodies, more connected to the world around them, and more equipped to handle life's inevitable challenges. There's no rush, no pressure to "fix" anything. Instead, we'll focus on fostering growth—gently, steadily, and with love. This is a process of unfolding, of learning to see the small yet significant changes that add up to meaningful transformation over time.

So, let's begin this journey with an open heart and a willingness to explore new possibilities.

Introduction

Why Somatic Therapy Matters for Children With Autism

Whether you're a parent, caregiver, or therapist, you've bought this book because you care deeply about a child with autism and are searching for ways to support their growth, well-being, and happiness. You may have already explored many different therapies, strategies, and approaches, and perhaps you're still wondering: *Is there something more I can do?* The answer is yes—and this book is here to introduce you to a powerful, yet gentle approach called somatic therapy, tailored specifically for children with autism.

Think of this as the beginning of a journey, not just for the child you care for, but for you as well. Somatic therapy is about more than addressing specific behaviors or challenges—it's about helping children connect with their bodies in ways that can foster calm, improve motor skills, and enhance emotional well-being. It's a holistic approach, rooted in the understanding that the mind and body are deeply interconnected, and that when we nurture the body, we also nurture the whole child.

This book is your guide, offering tools and insights to help you better understand how to use somatic therapy in a way that fits naturally into your child's life. Whether you're a parent looking to try simple exercises at home, a caregiver wanting to support a child in everyday activities, or a therapist eager to expand your toolkit, this book is for you. We'll explore how these body-based techniques can help children feel more grounded, more in tune with their surroundings, and better equipped to manage the sensory overload and anxiety that can come with being on the autism spectrum.

The goal here isn't to "fix" or change your child. It's about offering them—and yourself—new ways of experiencing the world. Somatic therapy provides gentle practices that help children develop a stronger sense of body awareness, which in turn can improve their emotional regulation, physical coordination, and overall sense of calm. And, as you'll soon discover, these practices are simple, adaptable, and accessible to everyone.

As you turn the pages, you'll find this book written in a conversational tone, like a friendly guide who's walking alongside you on this journey. You won't find heavy medical jargon or overwhelming details. Instead, you'll find encouragement, compassion, and practical tips that can be easily integrated into daily life. This journey is about progress, not perfection. We're here to help children with autism feel more at home in their bodies, and to give you, as their supporter, the confidence to help them along the way.

So, take a deep breath, and let's begin this journey together. There will be challenges, of course, but there will also be moments of joy, connection, and growth. This book is a resource for those moments, offering guidance and support as you help the child in your life thrive in ways you may not have thought possible.

Welcome to this adventure. We're so glad you're here.

Understanding the Connection Between Body and Mind

The connection between the body and mind is a fascinating and complex relationship that plays a significant role in how we experience and navigate the world around us. For children with autism, this connection can often feel out of sync, leading to challenges that go beyond what meets the eye. These children may experience emotional, sensory, and motor difficulties that are deeply intertwined, creating a cycle of overwhelm and frustration. This is where somatic therapy can step in as a powerful and holistic approach. By addressing the body and mind together, somatic therapy offers children with autism a way to reconnect with themselves in a way that feels safe, gentle, and empowering.

The Body-Mind Connection: A Foundation

To truly understand why somatic therapy is so beneficial for children with autism, it's important to first grasp the nature of the body-mind connection. Our bodies and minds are not separate entities functioning independently. Rather, they work together as an integrated system, constantly sending and receiving signals to help us interpret and respond to our environment. This relationship can be seen in countless ways—when we feel nervous, our hearts race; when we are joyful, our bodies feel light and energized. This is the mind-body loop in action.

For children with autism, this connection between body and mind can become misaligned. Sensory inputs—such as sights, sounds, textures, and even smells—may overwhelm their nervous systems, causing them to either shut down or become hyper-responsive. Emotionally, this overstimulation can lead to feelings of anxiety, frustration, or even rage. At the same time, motor skills might be affected, making it difficult for them to physically navigate the world with ease. Everything is interconnected, and when one part of this system is out of balance, it can trigger a cascade of challenges that impact the child's ability to function comfortably.

Emotional, Sensory, and Motor Challenges: How They're Interconnected

Let's break down how these emotional, sensory, and motor challenges are connected for children with autism.

Sensory Overload and Emotional Reactions

Children with autism often experience heightened sensitivity to sensory input. This means that a sound that seems normal to someone else—like a ticking clock or a vacuum cleaner—can feel unbearably loud and intrusive. Similarly, lights may appear too bright, or certain fabrics may feel unbearably rough against their skin. This sensory overload can trigger immediate emotional reactions, ranging from anxiety and fear to frustration or anger. Imagine being in a situation where everything around you feels too intense—this is often what children with autism are experiencing.

These emotional responses are the body's way of trying to cope with the overwhelming sensory input. The brain interprets these sensations as threats, and the child's nervous system goes into overdrive, preparing for a "fight or flight" response. Unfortunately, in situations where the sensory stimuli are constant or unavoidable, like in a classroom or a busy shopping mall, the child may not be able to escape or fight back. This can lead to meltdowns, withdrawal, or an ongoing sense of anxiety and tension.

Motor Challenges and Emotional Disconnection

In addition to sensory overload, many children with autism face motor challenges. These difficulties can range from fine motor issues, like struggling to hold a pencil or button a shirt, to larger gross motor challenges, such as difficulty with balance, coordination, or spatial awareness. In some cases, children may have a hard time making their bodies move in the way they want them to, even when they know exactly what they want to do. This can be deeply frustrating and can lead to a sense of disconnection from their bodies.

When a child feels disconnected from their body, it affects their emotional state. They may become discouraged or anxious, feeling as though they lack control over their movements or their environment. For instance, a child who struggles with motor coordination may avoid participating in group activities at school, not because they don't want to, but because they fear failing or being ridiculed. This emotional strain only adds to the stress of managing their motor difficulties.

The Feedback Loop of Stress

When sensory overload and motor challenges combine, they create a feedback loop of stress. A child may become anxious because of sensory overstimulation, which in turn affects their motor coordination. For example, if a child is overwhelmed by the noise and lights of a crowded room, they may find it harder to walk steadily or perform a simple task like picking up a toy. The frustration of not being able to control their movements then amplifies their emotional distress, which makes it even harder for them to regain control over their body.

This feedback loop can be exhausting for both the child and the caregivers. It can also be isolating, as children may withdraw from social interactions, school activities, and even family events in an attempt to avoid the sensory and motor challenges that seem insurmountable.

How Somatic Therapy Addresses These Challenges Holistically

Somatic therapy steps in to break this cycle of stress by addressing the body-mind connection at its core. Instead of focusing solely on behaviors or cognitive processing, somatic therapy works with the body to release tension, increase body awareness, and create a sense of safety and calm. This, in turn, helps regulate the nervous system, which can have a profound effect on emotional well-being, sensory processing, and motor coordination.

Releasing Tension and Creating Safety

One of the primary goals of somatic therapy is to help children release physical tension that may be stored in their bodies. Often, children with autism carry a lot of tension, whether from the stress of sensory overload, the frustration of motor difficulties, or the emotional strain of trying to navigate a world that feels unpredictable. This tension can manifest in tight muscles, shallow breathing, or even rigid postures.

Somatic therapy uses gentle movements and exercises to help children become aware of where they're holding tension and to release it in a safe and supportive way. For example, a therapist might guide a child through simple stretches or slow, mindful movements that encourage relaxation. Over time, these practices can help children feel more at ease in their bodies, which can reduce their overall stress levels and improve their emotional resilience.

Building Body Awareness and Emotional Regulation

Another key aspect of somatic therapy is building body awareness. Many children with autism struggle with interoception, which is the ability to sense what's happening inside their own bodies. This can make it difficult for them to identify when they're hungry, tired, or anxious. By helping children tune into their physical sensations, somatic therapy strengthens their connection to their bodies and enhances their ability to regulate their emotions.

For instance, a child might learn to recognize the early signs of tension building up in their shoulders or jaw. Once they're aware of these sensations, they can use calming techniques like deep breathing or gentle stretching to release the tension before it escalates into a meltdown. This kind of body awareness not only helps children feel more in control of their emotions, but it also gives them tools to manage stress in a proactive way.

Improving Motor Skills Through Movement

Somatic therapy also directly addresses motor challenges by incorporating specific exercises designed to improve coordination, balance, and spatial awareness. These movements are often slow and deliberate, allowing the child to focus on the quality of their movement rather than the outcome. This can be especially helpful for children who struggle with motor planning, as it gives them the time and space to practice new movements in a low-pressure environment.

One technique often used in somatic therapy is called "body scanning." In this exercise, the therapist guides the child's attention to different parts of their body, encouraging them to notice how each part feels and moves. This increased awareness can lead to greater control over their movements and a better understanding of how their body interacts with the world around them.

Over time, these movement-based practices can help children build strength, improve their coordination, and feel more confident in their physical abilities. This boost in motor skills can have a ripple effect, increasing their willingness to engage in social and physical activities that they might have previously avoided.

Regulating the Nervous System

At the heart of somatic therapy is the goal of regulating the nervous system. For children with autism, the nervous system is often in a state of hyperarousal, which can make it difficult to calm down once they've become overstimulated. Somatic therapy uses techniques like deep breathing, rhythmic movement, and grounding exercises to help children shift from a state of stress to a state of relaxation.

For example, a therapist might teach a child how to use slow, deep breaths to calm their racing heart when they start to feel anxious. They might also use rocking or rhythmic movements to soothe the child's nervous system when they're feeling overwhelmed. These techniques help to reset the nervous system, creating a sense of safety and calm that can carry over into the child's everyday life.

To make this more tangible, let's look at a few real-world examples of how somatic therapy can make a difference for children with autism.

Imagine a child named Liam who often struggles with sensory overload in noisy environments. At school, he finds it difficult to focus because the sounds of other children talking and the fluorescent lights buzzing overhead make him feel anxious. His teacher has noticed that when Liam becomes overwhelmed, he also has a harder time with tasks that require fine motor skills, like writing or cutting with scissors.

Through somatic therapy, Liam learns to recognize the early signs of sensory overload—his heart starts to race, and his shoulders tense up. His therapist teaches him to take deep, calming breaths and to gently stretch his arms and shoulders when he feels this tension building. Over time, Liam becomes better at managing his anxiety before it escalates, and his fine motor skills improve as a result.

Now, let's consider another child, Ava, who struggles with motor coordination. She often feels clumsy and unsteady on her feet, which makes her reluctant to participate in physical activities with her peers. This affects her emotionally as well, as she begins to feel isolated and self-conscious.

In her somatic therapy sessions, Ava practices slow, mindful movements that help her develop a stronger sense of balance and coordination. Her therapist might guide her through simple exercises like walking heel-to-toe or balancing on one foot. As Ava becomes more confident in her movements, she starts to feel more comfortable joining in with group activities at school. This, in turn, boosts her self-esteem and helps her feel more connected to her peers.

In both of these examples, we see how somatic therapy addresses the interconnected nature of emotional, sensory, and motor challenges in children with autism. By working with the body to release tension, build awareness, and regulate the nervous system, somatic therapy offers a holistic path to well-being. It empowers children to reconnect with their bodies in a way

How Somatic Therapy Can Make a Difference in Your Child's Life

Somatic therapy offers a profoundly transformative approach for children with autism, tapping into the body's inherent wisdom to foster emotional regulation, improve motor skills, enhance sensory processing, and promote overall well-being. As a body-based practice, it encourages children to explore their physical sensations and movements in ways that are accessible and non-invasive. For children on the autism spectrum, who often face heightened sensory challenges and difficulty processing emotions, this therapy offers a path toward greater calm, balance, and connection with their own bodies.

At the heart of somatic therapy is the understanding that the body and mind are not separate entities. The emotions we feel, the way we process information, and the way we move are all deeply interconnected. For a child with autism, emotional regulation can often feel like an overwhelming task. Their bodies may be in a near-constant state of heightened arousal, making it difficult to find calm, especially when faced with sensory overload. Imagine a child who becomes overstimulated in a loud, bright environment, their body tensing up, heart racing, and breath becoming shallow and rapid. In such moments, the body is reacting to stress in real-time, and without the tools to self-regulate, this child may experience a meltdown or shut down entirely. Somatic therapy steps in as a means to help these children become more aware of their physical sensations and responses to stimuli, allowing them to find ways to soothe themselves before the overwhelm reaches a peak.

For example, through simple grounding exercises, children can learn to reconnect with their body and find a sense of stability. A child might be guided to focus on their feet planted firmly on the ground, noticing the sensation of their weight pressing down, or they might be encouraged to gently rock back and forth to find a rhythm that brings comfort. These subtle, intentional movements offer a safe way for the child to bring their nervous system back into balance. As they practice these techniques, they start to develop a deeper sense of bodily awareness, noticing early signs of agitation and learning how to intervene before emotional escalation occurs. Over time, this awareness translates into improved emotional regulation, as children become more adept at managing their feelings in ways that feel manageable and within their control.

Motor skills, another area that somatic therapy addresses, are often a significant challenge for children with autism. Many experience delays or difficulties with both fine and gross motor coordination, which can affect everything from holding a pencil to running and jumping. These struggles are not simply a result of poor muscle development but often stem from a disconnect between the brain and body—a lack of awareness of how their body moves and occupies space. Somatic therapy can help bridge this gap by offering movement-based practices that encourage a greater connection between the brain and body.

Imagine a child who has difficulty with hand-eye coordination, struggling to grasp objects or engage in tasks that require precise motor control. Through somatic therapy, this child might be guided through activities that involve slow, mindful movements—like reaching for a toy in a controlled, deliberate manner, or practicing the sensation of squeezing and releasing their hands. By focusing attention on how their body moves, and breaking down these movements into smaller, more manageable steps, the child can build a stronger sense of body awareness. As they continue to engage in these somatic exercises, their motor skills begin to improve naturally, not through force or repetition, but through a growing understanding of how their body works. This gradual improvement in motor coordination can translate into increased confidence and independence, whether it's in playing with peers, participating in school activities, or simply navigating their daily routine.

Beyond motor skills, sensory processing is another critical area where somatic therapy can make a significant impact. Children with autism often face difficulties in processing sensory input, which can range from being hypersensitive to sounds, textures, and lights, to being hyposensitive and seeking out strong sensory experiences. These sensory challenges can lead to overwhelming reactions to everyday stimuli, making it hard for a child to feel comfortable and at ease in their surroundings. Somatic therapy addresses these sensory processing issues by offering a gentle, body-focused approach that helps children tune into their sensory experiences in a manageable way.

In a typical session, a therapist might introduce soft, soothing textures or calming movements to help the child explore their sensory thresholds in a safe, controlled environment. For a child who is hypersensitive to touch, for example, somatic therapy might involve gradually increasing their comfort with different sensations—perhaps starting with a soft fabric or a gentle breeze on their skin—while encouraging them to notice their body's reactions. By gently guiding the child through these sensory experiences, the therapist helps them build tolerance and reduce sensory overwhelm. On the other hand, for children who crave sensory input, somatic therapy might incorporate more active movements, like rolling on the floor or swinging in a hammock, which allows them to fulfill their sensory needs in a structured and calming manner. Through these practices, children with autism can begin to regulate their sensory experiences more effectively, which can lead to greater comfort in a wider range of environments.

Consider the case of a child who becomes highly agitated in crowded spaces, their body reacting intensely to the noise and movement around them. Through somatic therapy, this child can learn to identify the early signs of sensory overload—perhaps they feel their muscles tensing, their heart beating faster, or their breath becoming shallow. The therapist might guide them to take a few deep, slow breaths, helping them ground themselves in their body and tune out the overwhelming external stimuli. By practicing this over time, the child develops greater resilience, learning how to manage their sensory sensitivities in a way that feels safe and manageable. This newfound ability to cope with sensory input can have a profound impact on their overall well-being, reducing the frequency and intensity of sensory-related meltdowns and allowing them to engage more fully in the world around them.

The benefits of somatic therapy extend far beyond individual skills, however. At its core, somatic therapy fosters a sense of overall well-being, helping children with autism feel more connected to their bodies, more at ease in their environment, and more capable of navigating life's challenges. This holistic approach nurtures the child's sense of self, building confidence and self-awareness in a way that feels organic and empowering. As children learn to understand and respond to their physical sensations, they begin to feel more in control of their bodies and their emotions, which can lead to improvements in self-esteem and emotional resilience.

Take the example of a child who has always struggled with intense social anxiety, their body freezing up whenever they're in a group setting or asked to engage with peers. In somatic therapy, this child might start by exploring small, incremental steps toward social interaction. The therapist could guide them to notice how their body feels in these situations—perhaps their chest tightens or their shoulders hunch up. By bringing awareness to these physical reactions, the child can begin to understand that these sensations are signals from their body, not something they need to be afraid of. Over time, the therapist might introduce gentle, calming movements, like rolling the shoulders or taking a few deep breaths, to help the child release this tension. As the child practices these techniques, they gradually feel more comfortable in social settings, learning that they can manage their body's responses to anxiety without feeling overwhelmed. This newfound sense of control can lead to greater social confidence, allowing the child to engage with others more freely and enjoy meaningful interactions.

Hypothetical case studies offer further insight into the diverse benefits of somatic therapy. Picture a child named Liam, who has always struggled with transitions, whether it's moving from one activity to another at school or shifting from playtime to bedtime at home. These transitions trigger a wave of anxiety for Liam, leaving him feeling out of control and often resulting in outbursts. In somatic therapy, Liam is taught to recognize the physical sensations that accompany his anxiety during transitions. He might notice his stomach tightening, his hands clenching, or his breath becoming shallow. The therapist works with Liam to create a simple movement-based ritual that he can use during these moments of transition—perhaps a gentle rocking motion or a series of deep breaths combined with pressing his hands against a wall for grounding. Over time, Liam begins to use these somatic techniques on his own, learning to self-soothe during transitions and reducing the frequency and intensity of his outbursts.

Similarly, let's consider the hypothetical case of Ella, a young girl who is non-verbal and experiences frequent sensory overload. Ella is hypersensitive to bright lights and loud sounds, which often leads to meltdowns in public places. Through somatic therapy, Ella is introduced to calming, repetitive movements like swaying or rubbing her hands together, which help her find a sense of rhythm and predictability when she feels overwhelmed. The therapist also creates a sensory-friendly environment in the therapy room, with dimmed lights and soft music, allowing Ella to explore her sensory experiences in a way that feels safe. As Ella practices these movements and becomes more comfortable with different sensory inputs, her tolerance for public spaces gradually increases. Her parents begin to notice fewer meltdowns when they take her to the grocery store or a family outing, as Ella now has tools she can use to regulate her sensory experiences.

The power of somatic therapy lies in its ability to meet each child where they are, offering gentle, accessible techniques that help them feel more at home in their bodies. Whether it's improving emotional regulation, refining motor skills, easing sensory processing, or fostering a greater sense of overall well-being, somatic therapy provides children with autism a pathway toward growth that honors their unique needs and experiences.

What This Book Will Offer You and Your Child

By exploring the principles and practices of somatic therapy, you will come to understand how this gentle, body-centered approach can unlock new possibilities for your child's growth and development. Somatic therapy, at its core, recognizes that the body is not just a vessel for movement, but a gateway to emotional regulation, sensory balance, and overall well-being. This book will guide readers in integrating somatic practices into their everyday routines, making them accessible and adaptable to their child's unique needs.

As you read through these pages, you'll be equipped with practical, hands-on techniques that go far beyond theoretical concepts. Whether you're a parent, caregiver, or therapist, you'll learn how to engage with your child's body in ways that help reduce anxiety, improve motor skills, and foster a sense of calm and security. We'll dive deep into the specific somatic exercises designed for children on the autism spectrum—movements and activities that can be easily incorporated into daily life without overwhelming schedules or added stress. These are techniques that focus on listening to the body, tapping into its wisdom, and using gentle physical touch and movement to help children feel more grounded and in control.

More than that, this book is here to offer emotional support for you, the reader, as well. Navigating the world of autism can be daunting, and it's easy to feel overwhelmed by the sheer volume of information and advice out there. This book is different. It's not just about providing you with another set of tools—it's about fostering a sense of empowerment. It's about reminding you that, as a parent or caregiver, you have an invaluable role to play in your child's journey toward well-being. With the strategies and insights in this book, you'll feel more confident, more equipped to handle challenges, and more hopeful about the future. You'll begin to see how small, mindful changes can lead to big, positive shifts in your child's life.

What makes this book truly unique is its focus on personalization. No two children with autism are the same, and no two somatic therapy journeys will look alike. This book embraces that reality, encouraging you to adapt the exercises and techniques to suit your child's specific needs, preferences, and rhythms. It's not about rigidly following steps; it's about learning to be attuned to what your child's body is communicating, and responding with care and compassion. As you develop a deeper understanding of how somatic therapy works, you'll feel empowered to create an individualized approach that respects your child's pace while helping them move toward greater balance, strength, and emotional resilience.

You'll also learn how somatic therapy can support your child's emotional and mental well-being, not just their physical development. For children with autism, emotions can sometimes feel overwhelming, and this book will show you how body-based practices can help calm the nervous system and provide a sense of safety in moments of stress or sensory overload. You'll discover how to help your child develop self-regulation skills, enabling them to feel more in control of their emotions and more comfortable in their own skin. Through somatic techniques, your child can build a stronger sense of internal security that will serve them in navigating the complexities of life on the spectrum.

Ultimately, this book is here to serve as both a practical guide and a source of hope. It offers more than just techniques—it offers a new way of thinking about therapy, healing, and growth for children with autism. The goal is to provide you with tools that are not only effective but also compassionate and respectful of the unique experiences your child faces. By the end of this journey, you will have a wealth of strategies to draw from, as well as a deeper sense of connection to your child's body, mind, and emotional world.

Part 1

Getting to Know Somatic Therapy

Chapter 1

What Is Somatic Therapy and Why It Works

Understanding body awareness and its role in somatic therapy opens up a world of possibilities for supporting children with autism. Body awareness, often referred to as proprioception, is the sense that allows us to perceive the position, movement, and action of our own bodies. It's like an internal GPS system that helps us navigate our physical space and understand how our body interacts with the environment around us. This sense plays a crucial role in somatic therapy, particularly for children with autism, who may experience heightened or diminished awareness of their physical and emotional states.

When a child has a strong sense of body awareness, they can more accurately interpret and respond to sensory information. This means they're better able to gauge how their body is feeling, where it is in space, and how it's moving. For children with autism, who might struggle with sensory processing and emotional regulation, developing body awareness can be a game-changer. It provides them with the tools to better manage sensory overload, improve coordination, and enhance emotional understanding.

Imagine, for instance, a child who is feeling anxious but isn't quite sure how to express it. Their body might be tense, their breathing shallow, and their movements jittery. By developing body awareness, they can learn to recognize these physical signs of anxiety. Somatic therapy helps them tune into these sensations, allowing them to identify when they're feeling overwhelmed and to employ calming strategies before their emotions escalate. For example, a child might learn to notice the tightness in their shoulders or the clenching in their fists when they're anxious. With this awareness, they can begin practicing relaxation techniques like deep breathing or gentle stretching to alleviate the physical tension, helping to soothe their emotional state.

Practical exercises that enhance body awareness can be both engaging and effective. One simple yet powerful exercise involves using a body scan technique. This exercise can be done in a quiet, comfortable setting where the child is encouraged to close their eyes and focus on each part of their body, starting from the toes and working up to the head. As they mentally scan each body part, they can observe any sensations they feel—whether it's warmth, tension, or relaxation. This practice not only helps children become more attuned to their physical state but also provides them with a sense of control and calm.

Another exercise that can be useful is called "body mapping." In this activity, children use large sheets of paper and markers to draw an outline of their body. They then label or draw different sensations they feel in various parts of their body, such as areas that are sore, tense, or relaxed. This visual representation helps them become more aware of how their body feels and can also serve as a tool for communication. For children who have difficulty expressing their physical sensations verbally, body mapping provides an alternative way to convey what they're experiencing.

Movement activities, such as gentle stretching or dancing, can also foster body awareness. Encouraging children to move in different ways—stretching their arms overhead, bending down to touch their toes, or swaying to music—can help them connect with their body's range of motion and develop a better understanding of how their body moves through space. These activities not only enhance proprioception but also help children develop motor coordination and balance.

Incorporating sensory experiences, such as using textured objects or engaging in activities that involve different types of touch, can further support body awareness. For example, using a variety of textured materials—like soft fabrics, bumpy balls, or sand—allows children to explore different sensations and become more aware of how their body reacts to various textures. This can help them become more comfortable with their sensory environment and better manage sensory sensitivities.

Body awareness exercises can be integrated into daily routines, making them a natural part of a child's life. For instance, incorporating mindful movement practices during playtime or using body awareness techniques during calm-down periods can help reinforce these skills in a context that feels enjoyable and relevant. The key is to make these activities engaging and accessible, ensuring that they align with the child's interests and developmental stage.

The benefits of improving body awareness extend beyond just understanding physical sensations. When children become more in tune with their bodies, they also gain a better grasp of their emotional states. They start to recognize how physical sensations are linked to their feelings, such as noticing that their stomach feels tight when they're anxious or that their body feels relaxed after a moment of calm. This connection between body and emotion is fundamental in helping children with autism navigate their internal experiences and respond to them in a healthy way.

By integrating body awareness into their therapeutic practices, children with autism can develop a greater sense of self-awareness and self-regulation. They learn to recognize and interpret their physical and emotional states, enabling them to manage stress, enhance coordination, and experience a deeper sense of calm. This process not only improves their quality of life but also empowers them to engage more fully with their surroundings and relationships.

As we explore body awareness and its role in somatic therapy, remember that the goal is to create a supportive and understanding environment where children can develop these skills at their own pace. With patience and practice, body awareness can become a valuable tool for helping children with autism thrive, providing them with the foundation for a more balanced and fulfilling life.

How Somatic Therapy Helps Children with Autism Connect with Their Bodies

Somatic therapy offers a unique and powerful way for children with autism to develop a more profound connection with their bodies, and this connection can be transformative in multiple ways. At its essence, somatic therapy is based on the understanding that our bodies hold valuable information about our experiences and emotions. For children with autism, who often experience heightened sensory sensitivities and emotional responses, learning to tune into and understand these bodily signals can make a significant difference in their overall well-being.

When children engage in somatic therapy, they are guided to pay attention to their physical sensations, movements, and reactions. This practice helps them become more aware of how their bodies feel and how they respond to different stimuli. For many children with autism, who may struggle with processing sensory information or have difficulty expressing their emotions verbally, this increased body awareness offers a new way to understand and manage their experiences. By focusing on sensations such as touch, pressure, and movement, children can learn to recognize and articulate their feelings in a more grounded and direct manner.

One of the most significant benefits of this deeper connection is improved emotional regulation. Many children with autism find it challenging to regulate their emotions, which can lead to outbursts or overwhelming feelings. Somatic therapy helps by teaching them to identify physical signs of emotional stress before it becomes too intense. For instance, if a child starts to feel anxious, they might notice a tightening in their chest or a clenching of their fists. By learning to recognize these early signs, children can use somatic techniques to calm their bodies and minds, such as deep breathing exercises or gentle stretching. This proactive approach enables them to manage their emotions more effectively and reduces the likelihood of emotional overload.

Another benefit is the reduction of anxiety. Anxiety is a common challenge for children with autism, often exacerbated by sensory sensitivities and the unpredictability of their environment. Somatic therapy provides tools to help them anchor themselves in the present moment. Techniques like mindfulness and body scanning can help children become aware of their anxiety triggers and learn ways to mitigate their effects. By focusing on physical sensations and using soothing movements or touches, children can create a sense of safety and calm that counters their anxiety. This physical grounding helps them navigate stressful situations with greater ease and confidence.

Improved sensory integration is another crucial benefit of somatic therapy. Children with autism often experience difficulties with sensory processing, meaning their brains may struggle to interpret and integrate sensory information effectively. Somatic therapy's focus on bodily awareness and movement helps children develop a better understanding of how their bodies interact with their environment. Through activities that involve different textures, pressures, and movements, children can become more adept at processing sensory inputs. This improved integration can lead to greater comfort and adaptability in their daily lives, making it easier for them to handle sensory challenges and engage more fully with their surroundings.

In essence, somatic therapy equips children with autism with a toolkit for greater self-awareness and self-regulation. By fostering a deeper connection with their bodies, they gain insights into their emotional and sensory experiences, which can significantly enhance their quality of life. This approach not only supports emotional well-being but also promotes a more balanced and integrated sensory experience, enabling children to engage more comfortably and confidently with the world around them.

The Science Behind Somatic Therapy: A Simple Breakdown

To understand why somatic therapy is so effective, it helps to know a bit about how our bodies and brains interact. Imagine our brain and nervous system as a vast network of highways and streets, where every thought, feeling, and physical sensation travels along specific routes. When we talk about somatic therapy, we're diving into this network, focusing on how the body's sensations and movements can influence our mental and emotional well-being.

Let's start with neuroplasticity, which is a fascinating concept. Neuroplasticity is the brain's incredible ability to reorganize itself by forming new neural connections throughout life. This means that the brain isn't fixed in its ways; it's always adapting and changing based on our experiences. When children with autism engage in somatic therapy, they're essentially giving their brains new experiences—different ways of interacting with their bodies and the world. This can help reshape how their brains process sensory information, manage emotions, and respond to stress.

The nervous system plays a crucial role here. It's like the control center for all the body's responses to the outside world. The nervous system has two main parts: the sympathetic nervous system, which is responsible for the 'fight or flight' response, and the parasympathetic nervous system, which helps the body 'rest and digest'. For many children with autism, the sympathetic nervous system can be overactive, leading to heightened stress and anxiety. Somatic therapy helps to calm this system down by promoting relaxation and balance. It engages the parasympathetic nervous system, encouraging a state of calm and helping the body feel safe and secure.

Body-based therapies work by connecting physical movements and sensations with emotional and cognitive processes. For example, simple exercises like gentle stretches or rhythmic movements can help a child become more aware of their body and how it feels. This heightened body awareness can then translate into better emotional regulation and improved coping strategies. When children with autism practice these techniques, they're not just moving their bodies; they're also learning to tune into their internal experiences and respond in healthier ways.

Another key aspect is how these therapies impact brain development. The brain thrives on sensory input and movement, especially during the early years of development. By engaging in somatic practices, children receive a variety of sensory experiences that stimulate brain growth and connectivity. This can enhance their ability to process sensory information more effectively and improve their overall cognitive functioning.

Overall, somatic therapy taps into the body's natural ability to heal and grow by fostering a deeper connection between physical sensations and mental processes. It's about creating a nurturing environment where children with autism can explore their bodies, develop new patterns of response, and build a stronger foundation for emotional and cognitive growth. Through this approach, we're not just addressing symptoms but supporting the whole child—helping them to thrive in a way that feels natural and integrated.

A New Way to Approach Autism Therapy

Somatic therapy offers a refreshing and innovative approach to therapy for children with autism, setting itself apart from traditional methods with its unique focus on the body's role in emotional and sensory experiences. Unlike conventional therapies that might concentrate solely on cognitive or behavioral aspects, somatic therapy delves into how our physical sensations and movements are deeply intertwined with our emotional states. For children on the autism spectrum, this means addressing their experiences from a holistic perspective—one that acknowledges the profound impact of body awareness on their overall well-being.

This approach is particularly valuable for children with autism, who often experience sensory processing differences that can make traditional therapy methods less effective or even overwhelming. Somatic therapy works with the body's natural responses, helping children become more attuned to their physical sensations and learn how to regulate them. It's not about trying to fit the child into a pre-defined therapeutic mold; rather, it's about tuning into each child's unique physical and emotional landscape and working from there. This personalized, body-focused approach can help children feel more grounded and secure, which can be especially important for those who might struggle with anxiety or sensory overload.

One of the most innovative aspects of somatic therapy is its emphasis on gentle, non-invasive techniques that respect and work with the child's natural movements and rhythms. Instead of pushing children to conform to certain therapeutic exercises, somatic therapy encourages them to explore their own bodies and discover what feels right for them. This can lead to a more positive and engaging therapeutic experience, where children feel empowered rather than pressured. It's about creating a safe space where they can explore their sensations and emotions at their own pace, which can foster a deeper sense of trust and safety.

Moreover, somatic therapy introduces a new way of understanding and addressing emotional challenges. Rather than focusing solely on verbal expression or cognitive strategies, it acknowledges that emotions are often felt physically and can be processed through bodily movements and sensations. This is particularly relevant for children with autism, who might have difficulty articulating their feelings through words. By working with their bodies, they can learn to recognize and manage their emotions in a way that feels intuitive and natural to them.

Incorporating somatic therapy into a child's routine can also offer a more dynamic and flexible approach to therapy. The exercises and techniques can be adapted to suit different environments, whether at home, in school, or during therapy sessions. This flexibility can be incredibly beneficial for children with autism, who often thrive in structured yet adaptable environments. By integrating somatic practices into everyday activities, parents and caregivers can help their children maintain a sense of continuity and stability, which can enhance the effectiveness of the therapy.

Another key innovation of somatic therapy is its focus on the connection between the mind and body.

This integrated approach helps children with autism understand that their physical sensations are not separate from their emotional experiences. For example, a child who experiences physical discomfort or tension might also be feeling anxious or stressed. By addressing both the physical and emotional aspects simultaneously, somatic therapy can help children develop a more comprehensive understanding of their experiences and learn more effective ways to cope with them.

Somatic therapy also emphasizes the importance of building a strong therapeutic relationship. Because it involves a deep, empathetic engagement with the child's physical and emotional states, it fosters a strong sense of trust and rapport between the child and the therapist or caregiver. This relational aspect can be particularly impactful for children with autism, who may benefit greatly from a supportive and understanding therapeutic relationship that validates their experiences and encourages their growth.

For parents and caregivers, somatic therapy offers a new lens through which to view and support their child's development. It provides practical tools and techniques that can be integrated into daily routines, offering a hands-on approach to enhancing their child's well-being. By learning and applying these techniques, parents and caregivers can feel more confident in their ability to support their child's emotional and sensory needs, leading to a more collaborative and empowered therapeutic experience.

In terms of measurable outcomes, parents and caregivers can expect to see several positive changes in their children over time. For one, children may experience improved emotional regulation. Somatic therapy helps them become more aware of their bodily sensations and learn strategies for managing stress and anxiety. As they become more adept at recognizing and addressing their physical and emotional states, they may show greater resilience in the face of challenges and an enhanced ability to cope with sensory overload.

Additionally, improvements in motor skills are often a key benefit of somatic therapy. By engaging in body-based exercises and movements, children can develop better coordination, balance, and strength. These improvements can lead to increased independence and confidence in their physical abilities, which can have a positive impact on their daily activities and overall quality of life.

Over time, parents may also observe enhanced social interactions and communication skills. As children become more attuned to their bodies and emotions, they may find it easier to express themselves and engage with others. This can lead to more meaningful connections with peers, family members, and caregivers, contributing to a richer and more fulfilling social experience.

In summary, somatic therapy presents a fresh and innovative approach to supporting children with autism, offering a body-centered perspective that complements traditional methods. By focusing on the mind-body connection, personalized practices, and a strong therapeutic relationship, it provides a holistic and adaptable approach to therapy that can lead to measurable and meaningful improvements in emotional regulation, motor skills, and social interactions.

Chapter 2

Children With Autism: Unique Needs, Unique Solutions

Children with autism navigate a world that often feels vastly different from that of their neurotypical peers. Their sensory systems, motor skills, and emotional responses are uniquely attuned, which can lead to a host of challenges that impact their daily lives in profound ways. Understanding these challenges is crucial for appreciating why somatic therapy, with its gentle and body-focused techniques, can be such a valuable tool for supporting their development.

Sensory processing is one of the most defining features of autism. Many children with autism experience heightened or diminished sensitivity to sensory stimuli. This means that a seemingly ordinary sound, like the hum of a refrigerator or the rustle of leaves, can be overwhelmingly loud or distressing. Conversely, they might not notice or react to certain sensory inputs that others would find significant. This sensory dissonance can lead to significant discomfort and anxiety, making it challenging for these children to focus, engage in activities, or even participate in everyday life. A child who is overwhelmed by sensory input may become withdrawn or exhibit challenging behaviors as a way of coping with their discomfort.

Motor challenges are also a common experience for children with autism. They might struggle with fine motor skills, such as using utensils or writing, or with gross motor skills, like running or jumping. These difficulties can make physical activities feel daunting and frustrating, impacting their ability to play with peers, participate in sports, or even manage daily tasks like dressing themselves. For a child with autism, coordination problems aren't just minor inconveniences—they can be major barriers to independence and self-confidence. The struggles with motor skills often intertwine with sensory issues, creating a cycle where sensory overload exacerbates motor difficulties, which in turn leads to more sensory sensitivity.

Emotionally, children with autism may find it challenging to regulate their feelings and respond to social cues. Their emotional experiences can be intense and overwhelming, yet they may struggle to express or understand these emotions effectively. This emotional turbulence can lead to frequent meltdowns or shutdowns, particularly in situations where they feel overstimulated or stressed. Navigating social interactions can be particularly daunting; understanding social norms and interpreting non-verbal cues requires a level of emotional processing and flexibility that can be difficult for many children with autism. This difficulty in emotional regulation not only affects their relationships with others but also their own sense of well-being and stability.

These sensory, motor, and emotional challenges impact virtually every aspect of a child's life. In the classroom, sensory overload can make it hard to concentrate, leading to difficulties with learning and social interaction. At home, struggles with motor skills and emotional regulation can create tension and frustration for both the child and their family. Social interactions, whether with peers or adults, can be fraught with misunderstandings and emotional stress, further isolating the child and potentially impacting their self-esteem. Each of these areas of challenge can compound the others, creating a complex web of difficulties that can be overwhelming for both the child and those who care for them.

Somatic therapy offers a tailored approach that addresses these challenges in a holistic and supportive manner. Unlike traditional therapies that might focus solely on behavioral or cognitive aspects, somatic therapy emphasizes the connection between the body and mind. By focusing on physical sensations and movements, somatic therapy helps children with autism develop greater body awareness and emotional regulation. Techniques such as gentle touch, mindful movement, and breathing exercises can help to calm an overstimulated nervous system, improve motor coordination, and facilitate better emotional processing.

A tailored approach like somatic therapy is crucial because it recognizes the individual nature of each child's sensory and emotional experiences. Rather than applying a one-size-fits-all solution, somatic therapy adapts to the unique needs of each child, providing them with tools and techniques that resonate with their specific challenges. For instance, a child who is highly sensitive to touch might benefit from techniques that focus on gentle, non-intrusive movements, while a child struggling with motor coordination might find exercises that promote balance and body awareness particularly helpful.

Moreover, somatic therapy offers a compassionate and respectful way to support children with autism. It's not just about addressing symptoms but about fostering a deeper connection between the child and their body. By helping children tune into their physical sensations and emotions, somatic therapy provides them with a sense of agency and control over their own experiences. This can be incredibly empowering, giving children the confidence to explore their world with greater ease and resilience.

In sum, understanding the unique sensory, motor, and emotional challenges faced by children with autism is essential for providing effective support. Somatic therapy offers a valuable and empathetic approach that can help these children navigate their daily lives with greater comfort and confidence. By focusing on the integration of body and mind, somatic therapy provides tools that are not only practical but also deeply supportive, addressing the whole child in a way that fosters growth and well-being.

What Works Best for Your Child

Creating a personalized somatic therapy plan for a child with autism is akin to crafting a bespoke suit—every detail needs to be tailored to fit the unique dimensions of the individual. This process involves understanding the child's specific sensory and motor profiles and adapting the therapy to meet their needs. Let's walk through how to create a plan that's both effective and empathetic, ensuring it resonates with the child's experiences and preferences.

Imagine embarking on this journey with a fresh perspective. Somatic therapy is deeply personal because it engages the body's natural rhythms and responses. This means that what works wonders for one child might not be as effective for another. To start, it's crucial to have a thorough understanding of the child's sensory and motor needs. Every child on the autism spectrum has their own unique way of experiencing the world, and their sensory sensitivities and motor skills can vary widely.

Begin by observing and documenting the child's sensory preferences and aversions. Some children might be particularly sensitive to certain textures or sounds, while others might crave more intense sensory input. For instance, a child who is sensitive to touch might benefit from gentle, calming movements that avoid direct physical contact, while a child who seeks out strong sensory input might respond well to more robust activities that involve deep pressure. Pay attention to how the child reacts to different types of stimuli and adjust the therapy to match their comfort level.

Next, consider the child's motor skills and physical coordination. Some children may have difficulty with fine motor tasks like drawing or manipulating small objects, while others might struggle with gross motor skills like jumping or running. A personalized somatic therapy plan should incorporate exercises that align with the child's current abilities and help them build strength and coordination in a supportive way. For example, if a child has challenges with balance, incorporating activities that improve their proprioceptive awareness—like balance exercises or gentle rocking movements—can be beneficial.

A key element in tailoring the therapy is to include the child's preferences and interests. Engaging a child in activities they enjoy can make the therapy process more enjoyable and effective. If a child loves animals, you might integrate movements that mimic animal actions, such as crawling like a bear or hopping like a frog. If they are fascinated by music, rhythmic movements or dances to their favorite tunes can be incorporated. This personalization not only makes the therapy more engaging but also helps build a positive association with the practice.

As you design the therapy plan, it's also important to create a flexible structure. Children's needs and responses can change over time, and the plan should be adaptable to these fluctuations. Start with a basic framework that includes a variety of activities addressing different sensory and motor needs, but be ready to modify it based on how the child responds. Regularly check in with the child to gauge their comfort and engagement, and be open to adjusting the plan as needed.

In addition to observing and adapting to the child's responses, involving other caregivers in the process can provide valuable insights. Parents, teachers, and other caregivers often have unique perspectives on the child's behaviors and preferences. Collaboration with them ensures that the therapy plan is well-rounded and considers all aspects of the child's daily life. It's also helpful to discuss the plan with other professionals who may be involved in the child's care, such as occupational therapists or pediatricians, to ensure a comprehensive approach.

Building a connection with the child is another essential part of the process. Establishing trust and a sense of safety can make a significant difference in how well the child responds to somatic therapy. Start with activities that are soothing and less challenging to build a foundation of comfort. As the child becomes more familiar with the process, gradually introduce more complex exercises. Celebrate their progress and encourage their efforts, reinforcing their positive experiences with the therapy.

Throughout the development of the personalized plan, maintain an open line of communication with the child. Encourage them to express their feelings and preferences about the therapy activities. This can provide invaluable feedback and help tailor the sessions to their evolving needs. It also fosters a sense of autonomy and involvement, which can enhance their engagement and willingness to participate.

Finally, remember that somatic therapy is not just about addressing specific issues but also about nurturing the child's overall well-being. The goal is to create a supportive environment where the child feels empowered to explore their sensory and motor experiences in a way that promotes growth and comfort. By focusing on the child's individual needs and preferences, you create a therapy plan that is both effective and compassionate, allowing them to thrive in a way that feels natural and fulfilling.

Creating a personalized somatic therapy plan is an ongoing, dynamic process. It involves keen observation, thoughtful adaptation, and a deep respect for the child's unique experiences. By approaching it with empathy and flexibility, you provide a foundation for meaningful progress and positive change.

How Somatic Therapy Can Address These Unique Challenges

Somatic therapy offers a unique and deeply impactful approach to addressing the sensory, motor, and emotional challenges faced by children with autism. This body-centered therapy focuses on the intrinsic connection between the mind and body, leveraging this relationship to foster healing and growth. For children with autism, who often experience heightened sensory sensitivities, motor coordination difficulties, and emotional regulation challenges, somatic therapy provides a tailored means to address these areas with compassion and effectiveness.

When we talk about sensory challenges in children with autism, we're referring to how they perceive and respond to sensory input from their environment. Many children on the spectrum experience sensory overload, where everyday sounds, lights, or textures can become overwhelming. Somatic therapy offers tools that help these children better manage and integrate sensory information. For example, deep pressure techniques are often used to provide a calming, grounding effect. This might involve activities like deep tissue massage or the use of weighted blankets, which can help a child feel more secure and less overwhelmed. These methods work by stimulating the body's proprioceptive system—the system responsible for sensing body position and movement—which can be soothing and help in reducing sensory overload.

Another somatic technique that can be particularly beneficial for sensory integration is rhythmic movement. This includes activities like gentle rocking or swinging. Rhythmic movement helps regulate the vestibular system, which is crucial for balance and spatial orientation. For many children with autism, integrating rhythmic movements into their daily routine can help them develop a better sense of balance and coordination, and can also provide a calming effect. For instance, a child might benefit from a daily routine that includes a few minutes of rocking in a rocking chair or swinging in a sensory swing, which helps in stabilizing their sensory experiences.

Motor challenges are another significant area where somatic therapy shines. Many children with autism struggle with fine and gross motor skills, which can impact their ability to perform everyday tasks and engage in physical activities. Somatic therapy uses specific techniques to enhance motor coordination and strength. One effective approach is the use of body-based exercises that promote body awareness and control. For instance, activities such as crawling through tunnels, jumping on trampolines, or engaging in balance exercises on a wobble board can help improve coordination and muscle strength. These exercises are designed to be fun and engaging while also targeting areas that need improvement.

They can be tailored to the child's level and gradually increased in complexity as their skills develop.

Additionally, somatic therapy incorporates techniques that focus on body awareness and proprioception. Activities like yoga or tai chi, adapted for children, can help enhance body awareness by encouraging children to pay attention to their movements and positions. For example, simple yoga poses such as "cat-cow" stretches or "downward dog" can help children develop better control over their bodies and improve their flexibility. These practices not only support physical development but also contribute to emotional regulation by promoting relaxation and reducing stress.

Emotional challenges are often intertwined with sensory and motor difficulties, and somatic therapy addresses these by fostering a deeper connection between the child's body and emotions. One key technique used in somatic therapy is breathwork. Teaching children to use their breath as a tool for self-regulation can be incredibly effective. For example, slow, deep breathing exercises can help a child calm down when they're feeling overwhelmed or anxious. Guided breathing exercises, where a child might breathe in for a count of four, hold for a count of four, and exhale for a count of four, can help regulate their nervous system and provide a sense of calm.

Another aspect of somatic therapy that supports emotional well-being is the use of mindfulness techniques. Mindfulness involves paying attention to the present moment without judgment. For children with autism, mindfulness practices can be adapted to include simple, body-focused exercises that help them tune into their feelings and bodily sensations. For instance, a mindfulness exercise might involve a child focusing on the feeling of their feet touching the ground or noticing the sensation of their breath moving in and out. These practices help children develop a greater awareness of their emotional states and can be particularly useful in managing anxiety and stress.

Play therapy is another valuable component of somatic therapy for children with autism. Through play, children can explore their emotions, develop social skills, and practice new behaviors in a safe and supportive environment. Somatic play therapy might include activities like using therapeutic toys, engaging in role-playing games, or participating in sensory-rich experiences. For example, a play therapist might use a sand tray to help a child express their feelings and navigate challenging emotions. The tactile nature of sand can provide a soothing sensory experience while allowing the child to explore their inner world.

Moreover, somatic therapy recognizes the importance of building a supportive and trusting relationship between the therapist and the child. This therapeutic relationship is crucial for helping children feel safe and secure as they explore and address their sensory, motor, and emotional challenges. By creating a nurturing environment where the child feels understood and accepted, somatic therapy helps foster a sense of trust and safety that can significantly enhance the effectiveness of the therapeutic techniques.

Incorporating somatic therapy into the daily routine of a child with autism can lead to meaningful improvements in their quality of life. By addressing the sensory, motor, and emotional challenges through body-centered techniques, children can develop greater self-awareness, improve their motor skills, and achieve a more balanced emotional state. The practical techniques offered in somatic therapy provide a toolkit for parents, caregivers, and therapists to support children in a way that is both effective and compassionate.

Ultimately, somatic therapy is not just about addressing specific challenges; it's about empowering children to connect with their bodies, understand their sensory experiences, and regulate their emotions in a healthy and constructive manner. By embracing these body-centered practices, children with autism can experience a greater sense of well-being and navigate their world with increased confidence and resilience.

Seeing Transformation Through Somatic Therapy

Imagine a little boy named Ethan, who at the age of six, found everyday life to be a series of overwhelming experiences. The sounds of a busy classroom, the buzz of fluorescent lights, and even the texture of certain foods would send him into a state of distress. Ethan's parents were deeply concerned, as traditional therapies seemed to offer limited relief. That's when they discovered somatic therapy.

Ethan began with simple, body-based exercises designed to help him become more aware of his physical sensations and learn to manage his sensory overload. For instance, he engaged in activities that involved gentle movements, such as swaying with the rhythm of calming music or using a soft ball for deep-pressure touch. At first, these exercises were met with resistance, but Ethan's therapists and parents were patient, creating a supportive environment where he could explore these new sensations at his own pace.

Over time, Ethan's journey through somatic therapy began to show remarkable results. His initial reluctance gave way to a newfound sense of calm and control. The sensory overload that once seemed insurmountable began to feel more manageable. He started to use the calming techniques he had learned to self-soothe when faced with overwhelming situations. His parents noticed a significant reduction in his outbursts and a noticeable improvement in his ability to focus at school. Ethan's story is a testament to how somatic therapy can provide children with the tools they need to navigate their sensory world with greater ease and confidence.

Then there's Mia, a young girl who struggled with coordination and motor skills due to her autism. Simple tasks like buttoning her shirt or playing catch with her friends were often challenging and frustrating for her. Mia's parents were introduced to somatic therapy as a way to enhance her motor skills through body awareness and movement-based exercises.

In her therapy sessions, Mia engaged in activities that were both fun and therapeutic. She practiced movements that required her to focus on how her body moved through space, such as balancing on a soft beam or crawling through a tunnel. These activities were designed not just to improve her coordination but also to build her confidence and sense of accomplishment. Mia's therapists worked closely with her to create a tailored approach that aligned with her interests, incorporating games and playful elements to keep her engaged.

As Mia continued with somatic therapy, the improvements were both significant and heartwarming. Her motor skills became more refined, and she began to approach physical activities with enthusiasm rather than apprehension. The coordination exercises that once felt like obstacles became sources of joy and pride. Mia's newfound skills allowed her to participate more fully in play with her peers, fostering a greater sense of social inclusion and happiness.

Finally, let's talk about Leo, who faced intense anxiety and frequent meltdowns due to his sensitivity to changes in routine. Leo's parents sought out somatic therapy as a way to help him manage his anxiety and find a sense of grounding amidst the unpredictability of daily life. The therapy focused on helping Leo build resilience and develop coping strategies through bodily awareness and relaxation techniques.

One of the key techniques used with Leo was deep-breathing exercises combined with gentle, rhythmic movements. By practicing these techniques, Leo learned how to activate his body's natural relaxation response, which helped him calm down during stressful situations. His therapists also introduced him to sensory activities like squeezing a stress ball or wrapping himself in a weighted blanket, which provided him with a sense of security and comfort.

The transformation Leo experienced through somatic therapy was profound. His meltdowns became less frequent, and he began to handle changes in routine with greater ease. The anxiety that once seemed overwhelming started to feel more manageable. Leo's improved emotional regulation not only enhanced his quality of life but also strengthened his relationships with his family and peers.

These real-life examples illustrate how somatic therapy can be a powerful tool for children with autism, addressing a range of challenges from sensory overload and motor skills to anxiety and emotional regulation. Each child's journey is unique, but the common thread is the positive impact that somatic therapy can have in helping them feel more at ease, more capable, and more connected to their own bodies and the world around them.

Part 2

The Emotional Side of Somatic Therapy

Chapter 3

Building Emotional Resilience Through Body Awareness

Body awareness is a powerful tool that can help children with autism navigate the complex world of their emotions by tuning into the signals their bodies are sending. For many children on the spectrum, emotions can be intense and challenging to articulate. By developing body awareness, these children can start to recognize and make sense of how their feelings manifest physically. This process can lead to greater emotional resilience, as they learn not only to identify their emotions but also to manage them more effectively.

One of the simplest ways to begin fostering body awareness is through mindfulness exercises that encourage children to pay attention to their physical sensations. For instance, you can introduce "body scan" activities, where the child is guided to focus on different parts of their body, noticing any sensations or feelings without judgment. Start with just a few minutes each day, perhaps before bedtime or during a calm moment, and encourage your child to describe what they're feeling in each area of their body. Are their shoulders tense? Is their stomach feeling tight? This practice can help them connect physical sensations with emotional states, such as noticing that tense shoulders might coincide with feeling anxious or stressed.

Another technique is to use "emotion and sensation cards." These cards can feature various emotions like happiness, sadness, or anger, paired with pictures or descriptions of corresponding physical sensations. For example, a card for anger might include a drawing of clenched fists or a red face. By using these cards, you can help your child match their physical sensations with specific emotions. You might ask them to select a card that best represents how they're feeling at any given moment, and then discuss what those sensations mean. This visual and tactile approach can make abstract emotions more concrete and understandable.

Incorporating movement activities can also enhance body awareness. Activities like "movement check-ins" allow children to use their bodies as a way to explore their feelings. For example, you might encourage your child to engage in different types of movement—such as stretching, jumping, or rolling on the floor—and then reflect on how these movements make them feel. This could be a playful way to explore emotional states while promoting physical activity. You could say, "Let's try some big jumps! How does that make you feel inside? Do you notice any changes in how you're feeling?"

Breathing exercises are another excellent way to build body awareness and emotional regulation. Simple breathing techniques, such as "belly breathing," help children focus on the rhythm of their breath and how it affects their body. You can guide your child to place their hand on their stomach and feel it rise and fall with each breath. Encouraging deep, slow breaths can help calm the nervous system and make it easier for children to process their emotions. Try incorporating breathing exercises into your daily routine or as a tool to use during moments of heightened emotions.

Creating a "calm corner" or a sensory space at home where your child can retreat to when they feel overwhelmed can also support emotional resilience. Equip this space with soft cushions, calming music, or tactile objects like stress balls and fidget toys. Encourage your child to visit this space when they need to take a break and reconnect with their body. This designated area can serve as a physical reminder to pause, breathe, and check in with their emotional state.

It's essential to approach these activities with patience and consistency. Building body awareness is a gradual process, and it's important to celebrate small victories along the way. Encourage your child to express themselves through art or journaling, helping them to further explore and articulate their emotional experiences. By combining these techniques with a supportive and understanding approach, you'll help your child develop a deeper connection between their body and emotions, paving the way for greater emotional resilience and well-being.

Somatic Techniques for Soothing Anxiety and Frustration

When it comes to soothing anxiety and frustration in children with autism, somatic techniques offer gentle yet powerful tools for emotional regulation. These techniques focus on connecting with the body's natural rhythms and sensations, helping to calm an overstimulated nervous system and provide a sense of grounding and stability.

One of the most effective tools in this regard is breathing exercises. Simple, focused breathing can have a profound impact on emotional state, especially for children who experience heightened levels of anxiety. Encourage your child to practice deep, slow breathing through their nose, allowing their belly to expand and then gently releasing the breath through their mouth. This technique helps engage the parasympathetic nervous system, which counteracts the stress response and promotes relaxation. You might start by making this exercise fun—use a favorite stuffed animal placed on their belly and have them watch it rise and fall with each breath. This visual cue can help them focus on the rhythm of their breathing and feel more engaged in the process.

Grounding techniques are another cornerstone of somatic therapy. These practices help children connect with the present moment and their physical surroundings, which can be especially calming during moments of sensory overload or emotional distress. One grounding technique involves encouraging your child to use their senses to connect with their environment. For example, you might guide them to feel the texture of different materials, listen to calming sounds, or notice specific colors and shapes around them. This sensory exploration can help anchor their attention and provide a soothing distraction from overwhelming emotions.

Mindful movements also play a crucial role in building emotional resilience. These movements are designed to be slow, deliberate, and focused on body awareness, helping children become more attuned to their physical sensations and emotions. Simple activities like stretching, gentle swaying, or slow, rhythmic walking can help your child release tension and improve their emotional state. For instance, you might introduce a movement game where your child mimics the movement of a favorite animal—like the slow, deliberate movement of a turtle or the gentle swaying of a leaf in the breeze. These activities not only engage their bodies but also provide a calming, predictable rhythm that can soothe anxiety.

Additionally, incorporating touch into your somatic practices can be incredibly grounding. Gentle, reassuring touch, such as a light hand on the shoulder or a comforting hug, can help regulate emotional states by providing a sense of safety and connection. This can be particularly effective if your child responds well to physical contact. You might also use weighted blankets or stuffed animals to provide a calming sensory input, helping them feel more grounded and secure.

It's important to approach these techniques with patience and flexibility. Not every technique will work for every child, and it may take some time for your child to become familiar with these practices. The goal is to create a toolkit of strategies that they can use to manage their emotions in a way that feels natural and comforting to them. By integrating these somatic techniques into their daily routine, you'll be providing them with valuable skills for self-regulation and emotional resilience that can support them throughout their life.

Remember, the journey towards emotional regulation is a gradual process, and each small step forward is a meaningful achievement. By focusing on body awareness and providing your child with these calming tools, you're helping them build a stronger foundation for emotional well-being and a greater sense of control over their experiences.

Simple Breathing and Grounding Exercises You Can Try Today

Breathing and grounding exercises are wonderful tools for helping children with autism feel more centered and calm. These techniques are simple, effective, and can be seamlessly integrated into daily routines. Below are some easy-to-do exercises, complete with step-by-step instructions and explanations of how they benefit the nervous system.

---

1. Balloon Breathing

Step-by-Step Instructions:

1. Have your child sit or stand comfortably with you.

2. Ask them to place their hands on their belly, feeling the rise and fall of their breath.

3. Instruct them to take a deep breath in through their nose, imagining they are inflating a big balloon in their belly.

4. Have them slowly exhale through their mouth, as if they are letting the air out of the balloon.

5. Repeat this process for a few minutes, encouraging them to visualize the balloon getting bigger and smaller.

Benefits: Balloon breathing helps slow down the breath and promotes relaxation by activating the parasympathetic nervous system. This technique encourages deep, diaphragmatic breathing, which can reduce anxiety and stress while improving focus and emotional regulation.

---

2. Five Senses Grounding

Step-by-Step Instructions:

1. Sit down with your child in a comfortable space.

2. Guide them through the following steps, encouraging them to focus on their senses:

   o **Sight:** Ask them to look around and name five things they can see.

   o **Touch:** Have them notice and describe four things they can feel, like the texture of their clothing or the surface they are sitting on.

   o **Hearing:** Prompt them to listen and identify three different sounds they can hear.

   o **Smell:** Ask them to identify two scents, if available, or to think about their favorite smells.

   o **Taste:** Have them focus on one taste they can identify, perhaps from a snack or drink.

Benefits: This exercise helps ground children in the present moment by engaging their senses. It can be particularly useful during moments of stress or sensory overload, as it helps shift their focus away from overwhelming stimuli and back to a calm state of awareness.

---

3. Starfish Breathing

Step-by-Step Instructions:

1. Have your child extend one hand in front of them, spreading their fingers wide like a starfish.

2. Ask them to use their other finger to trace around the edges of their outstretched hand.

3. Instruct them to breathe in deeply as they trace up the outside of their thumb.

4. As they trace down the inside of their thumb, have them exhale slowly.

5. Continue tracing each finger, coordinating the breath with the movement.

Benefits: Starfish breathing combines deep breathing with gentle hand movements, which can help children focus their attention and regulate their emotions. This technique encourages slow, deliberate breathing, which can calm the nervous system and promote a sense of relaxation.

---

4. Rainbow Breathing

Step-by-Step Instructions:

1. Have your child sit or stand comfortably.

2. Ask them to imagine they are holding a large, colorful rainbow in their hands.

3. Instruct them to breathe in slowly and deeply as they visualize the rainbow expanding and filling with color.

4. Have them exhale gently, visualizing the colors slowly fading back into the rainbow.

5. Repeat several times, encouraging them to feel the calming effect of the rainbow's colors.

Benefits: Rainbow breathing uses visualization to help children connect with their breath in a calming way. The colorful imagery can make the exercise more engaging and enjoyable, while the slow, deep breathing helps soothe the nervous system and reduce stress.

---

5. Toe Wiggle Grounding

Step-by-Step Instructions:

1. Have your child sit or stand with their shoes off if possible.

2. Ask them to focus on their toes and gently wiggle them.

3. Encourage them to pay attention to the sensation of their toes moving and the feeling of their feet making contact with the ground.

4. Have them take slow, deep breaths as they continue to wiggle their toes.

5. Continue for a few minutes, letting them relax and focus on the sensation of their feet.

Benefits: Toe wiggle grounding is a simple yet effective way to help children feel more connected to their bodies and the present moment. This exercise engages the senses of touch and proprioception, which can enhance body awareness and provide a calming effect.

These exercises are designed to be easy to integrate into daily routines and can be tailored to fit your child's preferences and needs. Practicing these techniques regularly can help create a soothing routine that supports emotional resilience and promotes a sense of calm and balance.

The Long-Term Benefits: A Calmer, More Balanced Child

Building emotional resilience through somatic therapy is like planting seeds in a garden that will flourish over time. For children with autism, who often face a whirlwind of sensory inputs and emotional challenges, somatic therapy offers a nurturing space where these seeds can take root and grow into something truly transformative. By focusing on body awareness and incorporating gentle physical practices into their daily lives, children can cultivate a sense of calm and emotional balance that becomes more pronounced and effective the longer they engage with it.

When we talk about emotional resilience, we're referring to the ability to bounce back from stress, adapt to challenges, and maintain a sense of equilibrium even when life gets tough. For children with autism, this resilience is especially crucial. They often experience the world in ways that can feel overwhelming—whether it's a barrage of sensory stimuli, social interactions that don't come naturally, or an emotional landscape that's hard to navigate. Somatic therapy helps by creating a consistent, reliable way for these children to ground themselves, regulate their emotions, and build a stable inner foundation.

Imagine a child who, at first, might struggle with sudden outbursts of frustration or anxiety. Through somatic practices, they learn to tune into their bodies and recognize the early signs of these overwhelming feelings. It's like developing an internal radar that alerts them to emotional turbulence before it becomes too intense. For instance, a child might start to notice that their breathing becomes shallow or their muscles tense up when they're feeling anxious. By practicing deep breathing exercises or gentle stretching regularly, they begin to counteract these physical signals, which in turn helps them manage their emotions more effectively.

Consistency in somatic therapy practices is key to this transformation. Just as muscles strengthen with regular exercise, emotional resilience builds with ongoing practice. Over time, the body learns to respond more adaptively to stress and sensory overload. The child who might have once been easily overwhelmed by a noisy classroom or a crowded room can start to develop a greater sense of control and calm. This doesn't happen overnight, but with persistent practice, the changes become more profound and lasting.

One of the beautiful aspects of somatic therapy is that it doesn't just focus on what's happening in the moment. It helps children build skills that carry over into various aspects of their lives. For instance, practicing mindfulness and body awareness can improve a child's ability to stay focused during school activities or social interactions. When they're able to calm themselves and regulate their emotions, they're more likely to engage positively with others, participate in group activities, and even handle the frustrations and challenges of daily life with greater ease.

Think about a child who regularly engages in somatic practices like body scans or mindful movements. Over time, these practices help them develop a heightened sense of self-awareness. They learn to identify and articulate their needs more effectively, which can lead to better communication with caregivers, teachers, and peers. This improved self-awareness and communication can be incredibly empowering. It gives children a voice in their own lives and helps them advocate for themselves in ways that were previously challenging.

Furthermore, the emotional resilience gained through somatic therapy can positively impact a child's overall mental health. Regular engagement with body-centered practices helps to lower stress levels and reduce anxiety. When children feel more grounded and secure in their bodies, they're less likely to experience the intense emotional highs and lows that can accompany sensory overload and social stress. This steady emotional state contributes to a more balanced and content outlook on life.

Parents and caregivers will often notice a gradual but significant change in their child's demeanor. A child who once seemed easily frustrated or anxious might become more calm and centered over time. They may develop better coping strategies for dealing with stress and become more resilient in the face of new challenges. This positive shift not only benefits the child but also fosters a more harmonious home environment. When children feel emotionally balanced, the entire family can experience a greater sense of peace and stability.

The long-term benefits of somatic therapy extend beyond immediate emotional regulation. As children continue to engage with somatic practices, they build a toolkit of strategies that serve them throughout their lives. These practices can be adapted and scaled as they grow, helping them navigate the complexities of adolescence and adulthood with greater ease. The skills they develop through somatic therapy can serve as a foundation for lifelong emotional health and well-being.

Ultimately, the journey of building emotional resilience through somatic therapy is about more than just managing stress or handling difficult emotions. It's about creating a lasting sense of inner strength and self-assurance. It's about helping children with autism feel more at home in their own bodies and more connected to the world around them. With consistent practice and a supportive approach, somatic therapy can truly be a powerful tool for fostering a calmer, more emotionally balanced life.

Chapter 4

Managing Sensory Overload with Gentle Somatic Practices

Sensory overload is a term that comes up often in discussions about autism, but understanding what it truly means and how it impacts a child's daily life is crucial, especially for parents who are trying to navigate the challenges of raising a child on the autism spectrum. At its core, sensory overload refers to a state in which the brain becomes overwhelmed by the input it receives from the environment. This can be anything from bright lights, loud noises, and strong smells to the texture of clothing or the feeling of a crowded room. For children with autism, the world can often feel like it's turned up too loud, too bright, and too fast, making it difficult for them to process and respond to the information flooding their senses.

In children with autism, sensory overload happens because their sensory processing system works differently than in neurotypical individuals. The brain, rather than filtering out unnecessary information or background noise, takes in everything at once. Imagine walking into a busy store, where there's music playing, fluorescent lights overhead, people talking loudly, and multiple textures and smells competing for your attention. Now imagine that your brain is unable to turn down the volume on any of it—it's all coming at you with the same intensity. This is often the experience of a child with autism. Every sensation is heightened, making it feel impossible to focus on just one thing. The nervous system becomes overstimulated, and when there's too much information to process at once, the brain goes into a state of overload.

What makes sensory overload particularly difficult for children with autism is that they often lack the coping mechanisms to deal with this overwhelming sensory input. While neurotypical children might instinctively cover their ears when something is too loud or look away from bright lights, children with autism might not know how to regulate their sensory experience in the same way. This leads to feelings of frustration, anxiety, and even panic, which can then trigger a range of behaviors that parents often find challenging to manage.

One of the most common responses to sensory overload in children with autism is what's known as a meltdown. A meltdown is not the same as a temper tantrum, though it can often look similar to an outside observer. During a meltdown, the child is not simply misbehaving or seeking attention; they are experiencing an intense physiological reaction to their environment. The brain is in a state of overdrive, and the child is trying to release the overwhelming energy in any way possible. This can manifest as crying, screaming, hitting, or even retreating into silence or isolation. The important thing to remember is that meltdowns are not intentional acts of defiance—they are the child's way of expressing their distress when they can no longer cope with their surroundings.

In addition to meltdowns, sensory overload can also lead to what's called a shutdown. While meltdowns are outwardly explosive, shutdowns are more inwardly focused. During a shutdown, the child may withdraw from their environment completely, becoming unresponsive, quiet, or immobile. In these moments, the brain is essentially shutting down non-essential functions to protect itself from further overload. The child might stop talking, avoid eye contact, or curl up in a ball, trying to block out all sensory input. For parents, shutdowns can be equally as distressing as meltdowns because it can feel like their child has suddenly become unreachable.

These experiences of overload, meltdowns, and shutdowns don't just happen occasionally—they can have a significant impact on a child's daily life. For children with autism, simple activities like going to school, visiting the grocery store, or even sitting at the dinner table can become overwhelming. Sensory overload affects not only their behavior but also their mood. A child who is constantly bombarded by stimuli they can't control or escape is likely to feel anxious, irritable, and fatigued. Over time, this can lead to avoidance behaviors, where the child begins to resist certain environments or activities altogether. They may refuse to go places where they've previously experienced overload or become upset at the thought of trying new things, knowing it might trigger another episode.

One of the more subtle yet impactful ways sensory overload influences children with autism is through their emotional regulation. When a child is overstimulated, their brain is using all its resources just to manage the sensory input, leaving little room for emotional processing. This can make it harder for them to express how they're feeling, leading to sudden outbursts of anger, sadness, or fear. For example, a child might become uncharacteristically aggressive when overwhelmed by sensory stimuli, not because they're trying to hurt anyone, but because their emotions are bubbling over without a clear way to be communicated. Alternatively, they might seem unusually detached or apathetic in situations where they would normally engage.

It's also important to understand that sensory overload doesn't just happen in response to obvious stimuli like loud noises or bright lights. Sometimes, it can be caused by more subtle triggers—like the feel of a certain fabric against the skin or the buzzing of fluorescent lights in the background. For children with autism, these everyday sensations can be just as overwhelming as a loud explosion. This makes it even harder for parents to predict and prevent sensory overload because it's not always immediately clear what's causing the distress.

Parents often notice that sensory overload affects their child's ability to participate in activities that other children enjoy. For example, birthday parties, school field trips, and playdates can become sources of stress rather than fun. The combination of new environments, unfamiliar people, and unpredictable sensory stimuli can create a perfect storm for overload, leaving the child feeling out of control. In these situations, the child might seem withdrawn or irritable, and parents may find themselves walking on eggshells, unsure of how to help. Over time, this can lead to feelings of isolation, both for the child and the family, as they begin to avoid situations that might trigger sensory overload.

Sensory overload can also interfere with a child's ability to focus and learn. In a classroom setting, for example, the buzzing of the lights, the rustling of papers, and the hum of chatter can all be overwhelming for a child with autism. When their brain is focused on processing all these competing stimuli, it's much harder to concentrate on the task at hand, whether it's listening to the teacher or completing an assignment. This often leads to misunderstandings about a child's abilities—teachers may assume the child isn't paying attention or doesn't understand the material, when in fact, the child is simply overwhelmed by their sensory environment.

At home, sensory overload can impact daily routines like mealtimes, bedtime, and getting dressed. Something as simple as the texture of certain foods or the feeling of clothes on their skin can trigger discomfort and lead to resistance or avoidance. Parents might notice that their child becomes upset when asked to wear certain outfits or eat specific foods, not because they're being picky, but because their sensory system is in overdrive. These daily struggles can be exhausting for both the child and the family, leading to frustration on all sides.

For children with autism, the world is often a sensory minefield, where everyday experiences can quickly become overwhelming. But it's important to remember that sensory overload is not a reflection of their ability or character—it's simply a difference in how their brain processes information. With the right support, it's possible to help children navigate their sensory environment in a way that feels safe and manageable.

Understanding sensory overload is the first step in learning how to support a child through these challenges. It's about recognizing that their behavior is not random or defiant but a response to the overwhelming stimuli they're experiencing. As parents, caregivers, and educators, the goal is to create environments that reduce sensory input where possible and provide strategies for coping when overload does occur. By learning to manage sensory overload, we can help children with autism feel more at ease in their own skin, more capable of engaging with the world, and more confident in their ability to navigate the sensory challenges they face.

Sensory overload is a deeply personal experience, and no two children will respond to it in the same way. Some may be highly sensitive to sound, while others struggle with visual stimuli or tactile sensations. The key is to observe and understand your child's unique sensory profile, so you can better anticipate what might trigger overload and how to prevent it. Sensory processing is a complex and often invisible challenge, but by taking the time to understand it, you're already on the path to making life a little easier for your child and creating a world where they can thrive.

Using Somatic Therapy to Create Calm in Overwhelming Moments

When a child on the autism spectrum experiences sensory overload, it can feel as though their entire world is closing in on them. The noises, lights, textures, or movements in their environment become unbearably intense, overwhelming their nervous system and making it difficult to function or communicate. In these moments, it can be heartbreaking to watch your child struggle, unsure how to bring them back to a state of calm. This is where somatic therapy can offer a gentle and effective way to help. Through body-based techniques, somatic therapy addresses the physiological responses that occur during sensory overload, helping to soothe the child's nervous system and create a sense of safety in their own body.

One of the most powerful somatic techniques for calming a child in the midst of sensory overload is the use of deep pressure. Deep pressure stimulation works by engaging the parasympathetic nervous system—the part of the body responsible for rest and relaxation. For children on the spectrum, this kind of pressure can provide a grounding effect, making them feel held and secure. Imagine the way a gentle, but firm, hug can bring a sense of comfort. In somatic therapy, deep pressure can be applied through various methods, whether it's a weighted blanket draped over the child's shoulders or a gentle squeeze of their hands or arms. The key is to ensure the pressure is firm but not overwhelming. This kind of physical input helps to interrupt the overstimulation caused by sensory overload, offering a soothing contrast to the chaotic input their nervous system is receiving from the environment.

Rhythmic movements are another incredibly effective somatic practice when it comes to easing sensory overload. Our bodies are designed to respond to rhythm—whether it's the steady beat of a heart, the rocking motion of a swing, or the simple back-and-forth motion of walking. When a child is caught in the throes of sensory overload, introducing gentle, rhythmic movements can help reset their nervous system. You might try rocking your child in a chair, slowly swaying back and forth with them, or even encouraging them to rock themselves while seated on the floor or in a hammock. The repetitive motion helps regulate their overstimulated senses, providing a predictable pattern that their body can attune to. For many children, rhythmic movements have an almost hypnotic effect, gradually easing the tension in their muscles and allowing their body to settle into a more relaxed state.

Grounding exercises are another core element of somatic therapy, particularly for children experiencing sensory overload. Grounding is about helping the child feel connected to the present moment and their physical surroundings, which can be difficult during an overload episode when their mind and body are overwhelmed by stimuli. Simple techniques like having your child press their feet firmly into the floor, or guiding them to slowly touch and explore objects around them, can bring their awareness back to their body and the here and now. You might invite them to hold a soft object or rub their hands along a textured surface, drawing their focus to how the object feels against their skin. These grounding exercises work by bringing attention to sensations that are calming, familiar, and safe—helping the child re-establish a sense of control when the world around them feels too chaotic.

Incorporating breath work into somatic therapy can also provide significant relief for a child in sensory overload. Deep, slow breathing has the power to shift the body's stress response, lowering heart rate, reducing muscle tension, and allowing the mind to follow suit. Teaching a child to take deep, belly breaths can be transformative during an overload episode. You might guide them by encouraging them to place a hand on their stomach and feel the rise and fall of their breath. It can be helpful to use simple visualizations, like asking them to imagine they are inflating a balloon in their belly with each breath in, then letting the air slowly out on each exhale. The key is to keep the breathing slow and intentional, creating a calming rhythm that helps override the anxious, shallow breaths that often accompany sensory overload. Over time, with practice, children can learn to turn to breath work themselves when they feel overstimulated.

Somatic techniques also emphasize the importance of sensory regulation through tactile input. Many children on the autism spectrum have a heightened sensitivity to certain textures, and sensory overload can sometimes be triggered by tactile experiences that feel too intense. During moments of overload, offering a calming sensory experience—one that the child finds pleasurable—can help recalibrate their senses. This might mean providing a soft, fuzzy blanket for them to wrap themselves in or encouraging them to run their fingers through a box of rice or sand. These tactile experiences should be soothing, offering a stark contrast to the overwhelming input they've been receiving. It's about creating a sensory sanctuary where the child can retreat, allowing their system to reset in a way that feels comforting and manageable.

One of the core philosophies of somatic therapy is that the body knows how to heal itself when given the right conditions. When we focus on providing calm, gentle input to the body—whether it's through deep pressure, rhythmic movements, or grounding techniques—we're helping to create an environment where the nervous system can begin to regulate itself again. This is especially important for children who may not have the language skills to articulate what they're feeling during sensory overload. Somatic therapy meets them where they are, addressing the body directly rather than relying solely on cognitive interventions that may feel out of reach in the moment.

Incorporating somatic therapy into daily routines can also serve as a preventative measure, helping to build a child's resilience against sensory overload. Regularly practicing grounding exercises, deep pressure techniques, and rhythmic movements can help children maintain a more balanced nervous system, making them less susceptible to becoming overwhelmed in the first place. By engaging the body in these calming practices before an overload even occurs, parents and caregivers can help the child develop a more regulated baseline, making it easier for them to recover when they do encounter sensory challenges.

For parents and caregivers, knowing how to use these somatic techniques can be incredibly empowering. There's something deeply reassuring about having tools at your disposal that you know can bring relief to your child when they're feeling overwhelmed. Instead of feeling helpless or unsure of what to do, you can offer physical, tangible support that helps your child feel more grounded and secure. These somatic practices are not just reactive—they can be proactive, woven into the fabric of daily life in a way that creates a more soothing and supportive environment for your child to thrive. The beauty of somatic therapy lies in its simplicity. It doesn't require expensive equipment or advanced training; it asks only for a willingness to listen to the body, to trust its signals, and to offer gentle, mindful interventions that honor the child's experience.

Ultimately, somatic therapy provides a way to connect with a child in sensory overload that transcends words. It allows you to speak directly to their body, to offer comfort in a way that feels safe and supportive, even when their world feels too big and too loud. By embracing these practices, you're giving your child the tools they need to navigate sensory challenges with greater ease, helping them build a foundation of calm and security that they can carry with them into the future.

Techniques for Deep Pressure and Rhythmic Movements to Reduce Overstimulation

One of the most challenging aspects for children with autism is managing sensory overload. Everyday environments can feel chaotic, with too much noise, too many bright lights, and overwhelming sensations. For these children, overstimulation can lead to heightened anxiety, meltdowns, or withdrawal. As parents or caregivers, it's not only important to recognize the signs of sensory overload but also to equip yourself with effective strategies to help your child navigate these moments with greater ease. That's where deep pressure and rhythmic movement techniques come into play. These simple, yet powerful, somatic practices offer a grounding way to soothe your child's nervous system and help them find calm amidst the sensory chaos.

Deep pressure techniques involve applying consistent, firm pressure to the body, which can provide a calming effect. For many children on the autism spectrum, this sensation mimics the comforting feeling of being wrapped up, similar to the security they may feel from a weighted blanket or a tight hug. When administered mindfully, deep pressure helps calm the body's "fight or flight" response, reducing stress and fostering a sense of safety. While some children may initially resist, over time, many grow to crave this kind of pressure as it provides them with the sensory input they need to feel more in control.

To start incorporating deep pressure into your routine, consider beginning with simple, gentle techniques. One effective method is to apply firm, steady pressure with your hands to different parts of your child's body. Begin by asking your child to sit or lie down in a comfortable position. Once they're settled, you can start by pressing your hands down gently, but firmly, on their shoulders. Move slowly, ensuring that the pressure is even and consistent. Hold your hands there for a few moments, allowing your child to feel the full weight of the pressure. Then, you can release and repeat the process on different areas of their body, such as their back, arms, or legs. Remember, the goal isn't to rush through the motions but to be present with your child, letting them fully experience the grounding sensation.

Another technique that can be particularly helpful is using compression garments or wraps. These provide sustained pressure, much like a firm hug. Compression vests or weighted blankets can be used at various points throughout the day when your child is feeling overstimulated or anxious. If your child is comfortable with the idea, you might also try swaddling them in a soft blanket, creating a cocoon-like environment that mimics the calming pressure they may need. Encourage them to lie still for a few minutes, and as the pressure of the blanket soothes their body, you'll likely notice a shift in their energy and demeanor.

The key to deep pressure is finding the right level of intensity that works for your child. It's important to communicate with them and observe their body language. Some children may prefer more pressure, while others might feel better with a lighter touch. Being attuned to your child's needs will help you fine-tune these techniques so that they feel supportive and not overwhelming. Over time, your child will likely begin to associate deep pressure with a sense of calm and regulation, allowing them to better manage moments of sensory overload.

In addition to deep pressure, rhythmic movement can also be highly effective in helping children with autism manage sensory overload. These types of movements help to regulate the nervous system by creating a predictable and repetitive pattern that the brain can follow, which can be especially grounding for children who are feeling overstimulated. Rhythmic movement taps into the body's natural rhythms, promoting relaxation, emotional regulation, and a greater sense of balance.

One simple way to incorporate rhythmic movement is through rocking or gentle swinging. If your child enjoys physical movement, you might consider sitting together in a rocking chair or using a therapy swing. Encourage your child to focus on the slow, back-and-forth motion, which can have an incredibly soothing effect on both the mind and body. For children who are feeling overwhelmed, the rhythmic nature of the movement creates a predictable pattern that helps the brain shift out of a heightened, overstimulated state and into a more relaxed and balanced mode.

Another approach to rhythmic movement involves slow, repetitive motions like bouncing on an exercise ball or gently tapping your child's body in time with their breathing. You can encourage your child to sit on a large, inflatable therapy ball and slowly bounce up and down in a controlled, rhythmic fashion. This creates a soothing, repetitive motion that helps regulate their body's sensory input. If bouncing isn't comfortable, consider doing small taps or squeezes on your child's hands, arms, or legs, following the rhythm of their breath. This syncs their body's movements with their breathing, helping them find a natural rhythm that calms both their mind and body.

Parents and caregivers can also introduce rhythmic movement through activities like walking or gentle dancing. While this may sound simple, walking with intention can be a powerful way to reduce sensory overload. Focus on creating a steady pace and encourage your child to notice the repetitive pattern of their feet hitting the ground. You can make this practice even more effective by walking together in a quiet, natural environment, such as a park, where the sensory input is soothing rather than overwhelming. Similarly, dancing to slow, rhythmic music can create a calming atmosphere, allowing your child to move their body in a way that feels comforting and free.

It's important to remember that, like with deep pressure techniques, every child will respond differently to rhythmic movement. What may work well for one child might not resonate with another, so it's essential to experiment and observe how your child responds to different types of movement. Some children may find it calming to swing or rock, while others may prefer the grounding effect of bouncing or walking. As you explore these practices with your child, you'll gain a better understanding of what helps them feel more centered and in control of their sensory experiences.

The combination of deep pressure and rhythmic movement provides a powerful toolkit for managing sensory overload in children with autism. These somatic practices help to restore a sense of balance in the nervous system by offering consistent, soothing input that helps your child feel more grounded. And while these techniques are incredibly beneficial for your child, they also serve as a bonding opportunity. Taking time to engage in these practices with your child helps to strengthen your connection with them, showing them that you are there to provide comfort and support during moments of overwhelm.

It's essential to approach these techniques with patience and consistency. Your child may not respond immediately, and that's okay. The goal is not to "fix" their sensory overload but to offer them tools that they can use over time to self-regulate and manage their sensory experiences more effectively. With practice, you'll likely notice that your child becomes more attuned to their body's needs and better equipped to handle the sensory challenges that come their way. And perhaps even more importantly, you'll be creating a foundation of trust and security, letting your child know that they are not alone in their struggles and that there are ways to find calm in the midst of sensory overload.

Helping Your Child Reclaim Their Comfort in the World

Somatic therapy offers a unique and transformative approach for helping children with autism reclaim a sense of comfort and safety in their environment. For many children on the spectrum, the world can feel overwhelming—a barrage of sensory stimuli that floods the senses, making it difficult to process or respond effectively. Everyday experiences that others might take for granted, like the hum of fluorescent lights, the sensation of clothing against skin, or the sounds of traffic, can become unbearable triggers. This constant sensory overload can leave a child feeling perpetually on edge, anxious, or even frightened, leading to meltdowns, withdrawal, or physical discomfort. Somatic therapy gently addresses these challenges by helping children become more attuned to their bodies, fostering a greater sense of grounding and control.

The beauty of somatic therapy lies in its simplicity. It's not about forcing the body into rigid postures or movements, but rather about inviting the body to feel safe within its own skin. By encouraging children to tune into their physical sensations, somatic therapy helps them develop an awareness of their bodies that is often missing or fragmented due to sensory overload. This awareness is key to navigating sensory challenges more effectively. When children learn to notice how their body feels in different environments, they can begin to recognize what triggers discomfort and what helps them feel more at ease. Over time, this awareness becomes a powerful tool for self-regulation.

One of the first steps in this process is creating a safe and supportive space where children feel comfortable enough to explore their body's sensations. For many children with autism, sensory experiences can trigger feelings of vulnerability or loss of control. Somatic therapy creates a calm, non-judgmental environment where children can slowly and gently reconnect with their bodies. Simple exercises, such as grounding techniques that involve feeling the feet planted firmly on the floor, or slow, rhythmic movements that mimic the sensation of swaying, can have an immediate calming effect on the nervous system. These practices help children feel more secure in their bodies, which in turn makes them feel more secure in their environment.

As children become more comfortable with these gentle movements and practices, they can begin to use them as tools for navigating moments of sensory overload. For instance, when a child is feeling overwhelmed by loud noises or bright lights, they can engage in a somatic practice like deep breathing or muscle relaxation to soothe their body and calm their mind. These techniques help slow down the body's stress response, making it easier for the child to cope with the sensory input that's causing distress. Over time, this practice of checking in with the body and using movement or breath to regulate emotions becomes second nature, allowing children to feel more in control of their sensory experiences.

An important aspect of somatic therapy is its focus on teaching children to recognize and respect their own boundaries. For children with autism, sensory overload often happens because their bodies are bombarded with too much input at once—sounds, textures, sights, and smells that they aren't able to filter out. Somatic therapy helps children learn to identify the point at which sensory input becomes overwhelming and gives them the tools to respond before they reach a breaking point. By becoming more attuned to the signals their body is sending them, children can begin to set limits that protect them from becoming overloaded. This might mean learning to ask for a break when things feel too intense or using calming strategies to ground themselves before sensory input becomes unmanageable.

Somatic therapy also emphasizes the importance of rhythm and repetition, which can be especially helpful for children on the autism spectrum. Rhythmic movements, such as rocking or gentle tapping, can have a soothing effect on the nervous system. These repetitive motions help children feel more centered and provide a predictable sensory input that is often calming in moments of overwhelm. For some children, the act of swaying or rocking back and forth becomes a self-soothing behavior that helps them navigate sensory challenges in real time. Somatic therapists encourage these movements and even integrate them into structured practices, giving children a reliable toolkit they can draw from whenever they need to calm their bodies.

Over time, as children continue to engage with somatic therapy, they begin to build resilience against sensory overload. This is not to say that they will no longer be sensitive to stimuli or that the world will suddenly become easier to navigate. Rather, they develop an inner strength that allows them to manage their responses to sensory challenges with more confidence. When a child learns to calm their body through somatic practices, they gain the ability to face previously overwhelming situations with less fear and anxiety. This newfound sense of control is empowering. It shows the child that they are capable of managing their environment rather than being at the mercy of it.

Another crucial element of somatic therapy for children with autism is its ability to help them reclaim a sense of agency. Often, sensory overload can make children feel powerless—as though they are trapped in a body that won't stop reacting to the chaos around them. Somatic therapy restores a sense of ownership over their bodily experience. Through mindful movement and breathwork, children come to understand that they have the ability to influence how they feel, even in challenging situations. This awareness fosters a sense of safety, not only in the immediate moment but also in their broader lives. They learn that they can rely on their own bodies as a source of comfort and stability.

Parents and caregivers play a vital role in supporting their child's somatic therapy journey. By learning the techniques themselves, they can help reinforce these practices outside of therapy sessions, integrating them into daily routines. For example, a parent might guide their child through a grounding exercise before leaving for school, or use gentle pressure and touch to help the child feel calm during a stressful outing. The more these practices are incorporated into everyday life, the more natural they become for the child. Over time, children learn to rely on these techniques instinctively, turning to them whenever they need to find comfort or regain a sense of control in a stressful environment.

Somatic therapy is not a quick fix, nor is it a one-size-fits-all solution. It's a process of gradual discovery, one that respects the pace and needs of each individual child. Some children may respond quickly to certain techniques, while others may take time to warm up to the idea of engaging with their body in this way. But the beauty of somatic therapy is that it meets children where they are. It's a flexible, adaptive approach that allows children to explore at their own speed, building trust in their bodies and their environment as they go.

Ultimately, somatic therapy offers a pathway toward greater comfort, safety, and resilience. It helps children with autism navigate a world that can often feel too loud, too bright, or too chaotic, offering them tools to ground themselves and reclaim a sense of calm. With patience and practice, somatic therapy helps these children feel more at home in their bodies and more equipped to face the sensory challenges they encounter each day. It's a process of coming back to the body, learning to trust its signals, and using movement, breath, and touch to find peace amidst the noise.

Part 3: Movement and Motor Skills in Somatic Therapy

Chapter 5

Moving Towards Confidence

Body awareness plays a crucial role in the development of motor skills, particularly for children with autism. For many children on the spectrum, understanding and controlling their own physical movements can be a significant challenge. This isn't simply a matter of learning coordination or practicing movements. At a deeper level, it's about connecting the mind and body in a way that allows children to experience themselves fully in the world. This connection, often referred to as proprioception, is the sense that tells us where our bodies are in space, how we're moving, and what we're physically experiencing at any given moment. When a child struggles with body awareness, their ability to navigate their environment confidently and safely is affected, making motor development a more complex process.

For children with autism, this lack of body awareness can manifest in several ways. They might appear clumsy or uncoordinated, bumping into objects or people without realizing it. They may have difficulty with tasks that require fine motor skills, such as tying shoes or holding a pencil. Even everyday movements like walking up stairs or catching a ball can feel disjointed, as if their bodies aren't quite responding to the cues their brain is sending. This disconnect can lead to frustration, both for the child and those supporting them, and can even contribute to a sense of withdrawal or anxiety. After all, it's hard to feel confident when you don't feel in control of your own body.

This is where somatic therapy steps in, offering a gentle yet transformative approach to improving body awareness. Unlike traditional therapies that focus on repetitive drills or exercises, somatic therapy invites children to slow down and pay attention to the subtleties of how their bodies move. It teaches them to tune into the sensations of their muscles, joints, and even their breath, helping them build a stronger internal map of where their body is and how it operates. Somatic practices ask children to explore their bodies in a mindful way, which in turn fosters a sense of control and ease over their movements.

As children with autism begin to develop greater body awareness through somatic therapy, several positive changes can start to unfold. One of the first is an improvement in coordination. When a child learns to listen to their body's signals, they start to develop a clearer understanding of how to move smoothly and efficiently. Movements that once felt awkward or disjointed become more fluid because the child is no longer operating on autopilot. They are engaged with their body in a way that allows them to make small adjustments in real-time. For instance, they might notice how shifting their weight impacts their balance or how adjusting the tension in their muscles changes the outcome of a movement. This heightened sense of bodily feedback enables them to execute movements with more precision and control.

Balance, too, is an area where somatic therapy can make a significant difference. Many children with autism experience issues with balance, whether it's difficulty standing still without swaying, challenges with walking in a straight line, or trouble transitioning from one movement to another. Balance is deeply tied to body awareness because it requires constant adjustments that happen below the level of conscious thought. Through somatic exercises, children learn to become more aware of the alignment of their body—how their head, torso, and limbs are positioned relative to one another. This awareness helps them feel more grounded and centered, which in turn improves their ability to balance, whether they're standing on one foot or running across the playground. Balance isn't just a physical skill; it's a foundation that supports everything from basic movement to more complex activities like jumping, climbing, or even dancing.

One of the most powerful ways somatic therapy helps children on the spectrum is by encouraging them to slow down and truly experience the sensation of movement. For many children with autism, everyday tasks can feel rushed or overwhelming, leading them to move quickly without full awareness. Somatic therapy teaches them to pause, feel their body in action, and notice how their muscles and joints respond. This deliberate attention to movement helps children learn to modulate their energy levels, which is essential for maintaining balance and coordination. It's a process of retraining the brain and body to work together more harmoniously.

Another key benefit of improved body awareness through somatic therapy is the strengthening of muscles, particularly those involved in posture and core stability. Many children with autism struggle with low muscle tone or poor posture, which can contribute to difficulties in motor development. Through guided somatic exercises, children learn to engage the deep muscles of their torso, hips, and legs, helping to build a stronger, more stable foundation for all their movements. As their muscles become stronger and more responsive, children begin to experience greater confidence in their physical abilities. They may find it easier to sit up straight, hold their balance, or maintain a steady gait. Strengthening these core muscles also supports better fine motor control, making tasks like writing, cutting, or manipulating small objects less daunting.

Beyond the physical improvements in coordination, balance, and strength, there's another aspect of body awareness that somatic therapy taps into—emotional regulation. The connection between body awareness and emotional well-being is profound, especially for children with autism. When a child feels more connected to their body, they often experience a corresponding sense of calm and security. This is because body awareness helps regulate the nervous system, allowing children to feel more in control of their emotions. For a child on the spectrum who may struggle with sensory overload or emotional dysregulation, the ability to tune into their body and use somatic techniques to calm themselves can be life-changing.

In somatic therapy, children are encouraged to notice how certain movements make them feel, both physically and emotionally. They might observe that a gentle rocking motion soothes them, or that stretching their arms overhead gives them a sense of openness and relief. These moments of awareness help children develop a toolkit of movements that they can use to self-soothe when they're feeling overwhelmed or anxious. By building this internal repertoire of calming movements, children gain greater control over their emotional states, which in turn supports their overall development and well-being.

Importantly, somatic therapy doesn't just help children with autism feel more confident in their movements—it also helps them build a stronger relationship with their bodies. Many children on the spectrum have a complicated relationship with their physical selves. They might feel disconnected, uncomfortable, or even fearful of certain sensations. Somatic therapy provides a safe and supportive space for children to explore their bodies without judgment or pressure. Through gentle, exploratory movements, they learn to trust their bodies, to see them as a source of strength and stability rather than confusion or discomfort. This shift in perception is incredibly empowering for children, giving them a new sense of ownership over their movements and their experiences.

As children with autism continue to engage with somatic practices, they begin to internalize the lessons of body awareness, coordination, and strength. These skills don't just stay on the therapy mat—they extend into every aspect of their lives. Whether they're navigating a crowded classroom, climbing a tree at the park, or simply walking through the grocery store, the improvements in motor skills, balance, and strength gained through somatic therapy help them move through the world with greater ease and confidence. This newfound physical competence also opens doors for social interaction, as children feel more comfortable participating in group activities or playing with peers. It's a ripple effect, where improved body awareness leads to greater social and emotional engagement, further supporting the child's overall development.

Somatic therapy, by enhancing body awareness, gives children with autism a chance to feel more in tune with themselves and the world around them. It's not just about improving motor skills—it's about fostering a deeper sense of connection to their own bodies, helping them move through life with greater confidence, strength, and grace. The journey towards better body awareness may be gradual, but with each step, children gain more tools to navigate their physical and emotional landscapes.

How Somatic Therapy Builds Balance, Coordination, and Strength

Somatic therapy exercises are a powerful tool for helping children with autism improve their balance, coordination, and strength. These body-centered techniques work by enhancing the connection between the mind and body, encouraging children to become more aware of their movements and develop a stronger sense of control. For children on the autism spectrum, challenges with motor skills are common, whether it's difficulty with fine motor tasks, struggles with gross motor activities like running or jumping, or a general lack of body awareness. Somatic therapy provides a gentle, intuitive way to address these issues, fostering physical and emotional growth in a way that feels natural and supportive.

One of the most significant benefits of somatic exercises is their ability to improve balance. For children with autism, balancing can often be difficult due to differences in proprioception, the body's sense of where it is in space. Somatic therapy directly targets this challenge by encouraging children to tune into the sensations of their body as it moves, helping them develop a stronger sense of equilibrium. For example, simple weight-shifting exercises—where a child moves their weight from one foot to the other while standing—can help them feel more grounded and aware of their body's center of gravity. Over time, as children practice these movements, they gain a greater sense of stability, which can translate into better balance in daily activities, from standing in line to navigating uneven terrain.

Another key area somatic therapy can enhance is coordination. Coordination is all about the ability to smoothly and accurately control different parts of the body in relation to one another, which can be a significant challenge for children with autism. Somatic exercises aim to break down movements into manageable, mindful steps, allowing children to focus on the sensations and mechanics of each part of their body as they move. For instance, an exercise that involves gently reaching the arms overhead while simultaneously shifting the legs into a wide stance can help improve coordination. The slow, deliberate nature of these movements helps children connect the actions of their upper and lower body, giving them a clearer sense of how their limbs work together. This increased awareness builds the foundation for more fluid movement, improving coordination not just in structured exercises but in everyday tasks like getting dressed, playing, or engaging in sports.

Strength is another area where somatic exercises can make a profound difference. Often, children with autism may struggle with muscle tone or weakness, which can make tasks that require strength and endurance more difficult. While traditional physical exercise can certainly help build strength, somatic therapy offers a unique approach that focuses on functional movement rather than isolated muscle training. The goal is to help children develop strength in a way that supports their overall motor skills, rather than simply focusing on building muscle mass. For example, exercises like "wall push-ups," where a child stands a few feet away from a wall and slowly pushes and releases against it with their hands, can be a gentle yet effective way to build strength in the arms and upper body. At the same time, it reinforces body awareness and balance, making it a well-rounded activity that benefits multiple motor skills simultaneously.

In addition to these more specific movements, somatic therapy often incorporates full-body exercises that engage multiple muscle groups and foster overall motor development. One technique that has shown particular benefit is "rolling," where a child is guided to roll their body from side to side on a mat. This movement may seem simple, but it activates the core muscles, improves trunk stability, and enhances coordination between the upper and lower body. Rolling also provides sensory input that helps the child become more aware of their body's position in space, a critical element for both balance and coordination. As children become more comfortable with this exercise, they can transition to more complex movements, such as rolling into a sitting or standing position, further developing their motor skills and physical confidence.

Another effective somatic technique for motor development is "cross-body movements." These exercises involve moving one side of the body across the midline to the opposite side, such as bringing the right hand to touch the left knee. These types of movements engage both hemispheres of the brain, improving not only coordination but also motor planning and spatial awareness. For children with autism, who may struggle with crossing the midline in their movements, these exercises are crucial for developing more fluid and integrated motor patterns. They can also be adapted to different levels of ability, making them accessible and beneficial for a wide range of children.

Perhaps one of the most empowering aspects of somatic therapy is its emphasis on building confidence through movement. As children engage in these exercises and begin to see improvements in their balance, coordination, and strength, they also develop a sense of achievement and self-assurance. The movements are designed to be gentle and non-threatening, allowing children to succeed without the pressure of competition or performance. This gradual, positive reinforcement helps children feel more capable in their bodies, which in turn can lead to greater participation in physical activities and play. For children on the autism spectrum, who may often feel disconnected from their bodies or anxious about physical tasks, this newfound confidence can be life-changing.

Somatic therapy doesn't just focus on physical outcomes, though—it recognizes the deep connection between the body and emotions. As children work through these exercises, they may also experience emotional shifts that further support their motor development. For example, as a child learns to balance on one foot or coordinate a series of movements, they may also feel a sense of calm or focus that helps regulate their emotions. This is especially important for children with autism, who often face sensory overload or emotional dysregulation. By helping children become more attuned to their bodies and develop greater control over their movements, somatic therapy can reduce anxiety and promote a sense of calm, making it easier for them to engage with the world around them.

In essence, somatic therapy offers a holistic approach to motor skill development that goes beyond traditional exercises. By focusing on mindful, body-based techniques, it helps children with autism improve their balance, coordination, and strength in a way that feels natural and supportive. These exercises are not just about moving the body—they are about fostering a deeper connection between the mind and body, helping children feel more at home in their own skin. And as they develop these motor skills, they also build the confidence and resilience they need to thrive in their daily lives.

Gentle Movement Exercises You Can Do at Home (With Step-by-Step Instructions)

Here's a list of gentle, somatic-based exercises that parents can easily do with their children at home. These movements are designed to help improve motor skills, increase body awareness, and, most importantly, foster a sense of connection between you and your child. Each exercise can be done in a calm, playful way that invites your child to explore movement without feeling overwhelmed. Think of these moments as opportunities to bond and create a safe space where your child can feel grounded in their body.

1. The Grounding Breath This is a simple exercise to help your child feel more connected to the earth and present in their body. It can be particularly helpful when they're feeling anxious or overstimulated.

- **How to do it:**

  - Find a quiet space and have your child sit on the floor, either cross-legged or with legs stretched out in front of them.

  - Sit down with them, mirroring their position, and gently guide them to place their hands on their belly.

  - Invite your child to take a slow, deep breath in through their nose, imagining that they're filling their belly with air like a balloon.

  - As they breathe out through their mouth, encourage them to release any tension, feeling the connection between their body and the ground.

  - Repeat this for 5-6 breaths, keeping the pace slow and calming. You can use a soft, rhythmic voice to encourage them to stay focused on the breath.

This simple exercise helps children tune into their breath, calming their nervous system while also building a greater sense of body awareness.

2. Gentle Rocking Rocking movements are naturally soothing and can help regulate the nervous system. This exercise is especially helpful for children who have difficulty sitting still or who experience sensory overload.

- **How to do it:**

    o Sit with your child either on a chair or on the floor with their legs crossed.

    o Gently encourage your child to rock their body side to side. You can start with very small, slow movements.

    o As they get comfortable, you can slowly expand the rocking motion, allowing their entire torso to gently sway.

    o You can add a verbal cue, saying something like, "Let's rock like a calm wave in the ocean."

    o If your child is open to it, you can place a light hand on their back or shoulder to provide extra support, letting them feel your calm energy.

This movement helps children feel a sense of rhythm and balance, which is important for motor coordination. It also has a naturally calming effect that can help reduce anxiety.

3. The Starfish Stretch This is a great full-body stretch that encourages your child to explore their body's length and reach, promoting both strength and flexibility in a fun and playful way.

- **How to do it:**
    - Have your child lie on their back on a soft surface like a mat or carpet.
    - Ask them to stretch their arms and legs out wide, like a starfish, and reach as far as they can with both their fingers and toes.
    - Guide them to hold this stretch for a few moments while they take a deep breath in and out.
    - After a few seconds, have them bring their arms and legs in toward their body, curling up into a little ball (like a tiny starfish closing up).
    - Repeat this motion a few times, alternating between the wide stretch and the small curl.

This exercise helps children understand their body's dimensions while improving flexibility and core strength. Plus, it's a fun way to get them moving without any pressure!

4. Balloon Pushing This exercise is perfect for developing coordination and strength while staying playful. It's a great way to engage your child in a gentle movement activity that doesn't feel like work.

- **How to do it:**
  - Blow up a soft balloon and have your child stand or sit, depending on what feels most comfortable for them.
  - Hold the balloon lightly between your hands and slowly push it toward your child, encouraging them to push it back to you.
  - The goal is to keep the balloon in the air without letting it touch the ground, but don't worry if it does—just pick it up and start again.
  - You can make this more fun by introducing light verbal cues, like pretending the balloon is a delicate bubble they must carefully push without popping it.

This exercise helps with hand-eye coordination, reflexes, and motor control, all while keeping the mood light and playful.

5. Animal Walks This is a fun way to incorporate movement and imagination, helping your child engage different muscle groups and explore new ways of moving their body.

- **How to do it:**
    - Choose a few animals that your child likes—such as a bear, frog, or crab.
    - For a bear walk, encourage your child to walk on all fours, with their hands and feet on the ground and their hips lifted up like a bear moving through the woods.
    - For a frog jump, have them crouch down low and then hop forward, pretending to leap from lily pad to lily pad.
    - For a crab walk, guide your child to sit with their hands and feet on the ground, then lift their body off the floor and "walk" backward, like a crab scuttling along the beach.
    - Encourage them to make the animal sounds as they go!

These playful movements build strength, improve motor skills, and encourage creativity. Plus, they're a great way for children to release energy in a fun, focused way.

6. Hand Squeeze Relaxation This simple exercise can help children feel more in control of their body, while also building fine motor skills and improving body awareness.

- **How to do it:**

    o Sit with your child in a calm space and invite them to hold one of their hands out in front of them, palm up.

    o Gently guide them to squeeze their hand into a tight fist, holding the squeeze for a few seconds.

    o After a moment, ask them to slowly release the squeeze, opening their hand up wide and relaxing the fingers.

    o Repeat this a few times, encouraging them to notice the difference between the tight squeeze and the relaxed, open hand.

This exercise helps children understand the sensation of tension and release in their body, giving them a sense of control over their physical state. It's also a great tool for calming down during moments of frustration or anxiety.

Each of these exercises is designed to be done with love and patience, meeting your child wherever they are in their journey. The key is to keep things light and playful—there's no right or wrong way to do them. What matters most is the connection you're building, the gentle encouragement you're offering, and the sense of safety and calm you're nurturing in your child as they explore their body and its movements.

The Power of Small Wins: How Progress Builds Confidence

The journey of improving motor skills in children with autism is often filled with small, incremental steps. These steps, while they may seem minor at first glance, are in fact monumental for a child's development. It's easy to overlook them in pursuit of larger milestones, but learning to celebrate these small achievements is crucial not only for fostering growth but also for building a child's confidence. When we pause to recognize and honor these "small wins," we affirm a child's effort and progress, sending the message that they are capable, that their hard work is paying off, and that they are moving forward in their own unique way.

In the world of somatic therapy, motor skill development doesn't happen overnight. It unfolds through gentle exercises that encourage the child to engage with their body, become more aware of their movements, and slowly but surely improve their physical coordination. Every time a child gains a little more control over their motor skills—whether it's mastering a new movement or simply improving balance—these moments are victories. A child with autism may experience challenges with gross and fine motor skills that make everyday activities, like buttoning a shirt or kicking a ball, feel daunting. When they achieve even the smallest improvement, it's a sign that their body is learning, adapting, and responding to the somatic exercises in meaningful ways. These small wins are a reflection of the body's capacity to grow, even if progress may appear gradual.

Celebrating these small achievements creates an environment of encouragement and positivity that is essential for continued progress. For many children with autism, learning a new motor skill can be challenging, often accompanied by frustration, anxiety, or a sense of failure when things don't come easily. When we celebrate the little steps—whether it's taking two steps instead of one, holding onto a toy a little longer, or maintaining focus on a movement for a few extra seconds—we shift the focus away from perfection and place it on effort and persistence. This shift allows children to feel proud of their hard work, even if they haven't yet reached the end goal. In doing so, we help them build a mindset that values progress over perfection, which is key to sustaining motivation and resilience in the long term.

Confidence is one of the most important gifts we can give to a child, especially when they are navigating the complex world of motor skills. Every time a child is recognized for an achievement, no matter how small, their sense of self-worth grows. They begin to believe in their own abilities, which in turn encourages them to try new things, to push through difficult moments, and to trust that with practice, they can overcome challenges. This belief in their own competence lays the foundation for future success, not only in motor skill development but in all areas of life. The more a child feels that their efforts are valued, the more likely they are to embrace new challenges with a sense of determination rather than fear.

In the context of somatic therapy, this focus on celebrating small achievements is particularly powerful because somatic exercises are inherently process-oriented. These exercises are designed to work with the body's natural rhythms and capacities, encouraging gentle, mindful movement rather than rigid goals. When a child is able to experience even a slight improvement in their motor skills—perhaps they can balance for a second longer or coordinate their hands in a more fluid motion—it's a sign that their body is responding to the therapy in positive ways. Acknowledging these moments reinforces the idea that progress is happening, even if it's not always immediately visible. The body is learning, adapting, and growing, and each small win is a tangible reminder of that.

This approach is also deeply affirming for parents and caregivers. It can be easy to fall into the trap of focusing on what a child has not yet achieved, particularly when faced with the pressures and challenges of raising a child with autism. But when we shift the focus to what the child *has* achieved, no matter how small, we create a more compassionate and hopeful perspective. It reminds us that growth is happening, even if it's at a slower pace than we might have hoped for. By celebrating these small wins, we not only uplift the child, but we also remind ourselves that every step forward is a step toward greater capability and confidence.

One of the profound benefits of recognizing small achievements is that it helps a child develop a sense of mastery. When a child learns to associate effort with success, they begin to internalize the idea that they *can* succeed—that they are not limited by their current abilities, but are capable of growth. This is especially important for children who may have struggled with motor skills for most of their lives. They may have internalized a sense of failure or inadequacy when it comes to physical tasks. Celebrating small wins helps rewrite that narrative, teaching them that their body is capable of learning and that with each practice session, they are moving closer to their goals.

This sense of mastery also fosters resilience. As children experience the positive feedback loop of effort leading to progress, they become more willing to face challenges. Motor skill development can be a slow process, but when a child understands that even small steps are meaningful, they are more likely to persevere through difficult moments. They learn to trust the process, recognizing that their body is on a journey of growth, even when setbacks occur. This resilience is invaluable not only in somatic therapy but in life, as it teaches children the importance of persistence and the rewards of sticking with something, even when it's hard.

Furthermore, celebrating small wins helps reduce anxiety and frustration, which are common emotional responses for children working on motor skills. For many children with autism, physical tasks can feel overwhelming, especially if they struggle with coordination or sensory integration. This can lead to feelings of defeat before they even begin. However, when we shift the focus to recognizing small progress, we create an environment where success feels more attainable. Instead of facing an insurmountable task, children begin to see that each attempt is an opportunity for growth. This reframing can reduce the pressure they feel to "get it right" and instead encourage them to explore their movements with curiosity and openness.

It's also worth noting that these small wins don't just build confidence in motor skills—they have a ripple effect on other areas of development. As a child becomes more confident in their body, they are likely to feel more confident in social interactions, academic tasks, and other areas where they may have previously felt insecure. Somatic therapy teaches children that their body is a source of strength, and that understanding naturally extends into other facets of life. When they feel more capable in their physical abilities, they are more willing to engage with the world around them, whether that's participating in a group activity, trying a new skill, or simply navigating their day with a greater sense of ease and autonomy.

The importance of celebrating small wins goes beyond the immediate moment of achievement—it creates a lasting impact on how a child views themselves and their ability to learn and grow. Every small victory adds to the foundation of their self-esteem, building a sense of competence and belief in their abilities. Over time, this accumulation of small successes creates a powerful internal narrative: "I can do this. I am capable. I am growing." This narrative becomes a core part of how the child approaches not just motor skill development, but every challenge they face. It's a gift that will continue to serve them throughout their lives, long after the specific motor skills have been mastered.

In celebrating these achievements, we offer our children more than just praise—we offer them the tools to build a resilient, confident, and capable self. Through somatic therapy, we are not only helping them develop motor skills, but also nurturing a sense of self-worth that will carry them through the challenges and triumphs of life. And that, ultimately, is the greatest win of all.

Part 3

Movement and
Motor Skills in
Somatic Therapy

Chapter 6

Encouraging Healthy Posture and Movement Patterns

Posture might seem like a simple concept, but for children with autism, it plays a crucial role in their overall development and well-being. The way a child holds their body can deeply influence their motor skills, sensory processing, and emotional health. By understanding and addressing posture, we can offer significant benefits that go beyond just looking straight or sitting up properly. Instead, we tap into a fundamental aspect of how a child interacts with their environment and their own body, which can lead to profound improvements in their daily life.

For many children with autism, developing motor skills can be challenging. This is often due to differences in how their bodies perceive and process movement. Good posture supports motor development by providing a stable foundation for movement. When a child maintains proper posture, they are more likely to move efficiently and with greater control. This means they can engage more effectively in activities that require fine and gross motor skills, from writing with a pencil to climbing on playground equipment. Poor posture, on the other hand, can lead to inefficient movement patterns and a lack of coordination. For instance, a child who slouches or leans to one side may struggle with balance and spatial awareness, which are essential for tasks like catching a ball or navigating through a crowded room.

The impact of posture on sensory processing is equally significant. Sensory processing involves how the brain interprets and responds to information from the senses—like touch, sight, and movement. Children with autism often experience sensory processing differences, which can make them either hypersensitive or hyposensitive to sensory stimuli. Posture influences how sensory input is received and processed. Proper alignment can help a child's body organize sensory information more effectively. For instance, a child who sits upright at a desk may find it easier to focus on a task because their sensory system is less likely to be overwhelmed by the physical discomfort of poor posture. Conversely, poor posture can exacerbate sensory processing issues. A child who is slumped over might experience increased discomfort and difficulty focusing, leading to heightened sensory overload and stress.

Additionally, posture affects a child's emotional state and overall well-being. Good posture is associated with a sense of confidence and self-assurance. When a child feels physically supported and aligned, they are more likely to feel secure and capable. This can translate into improved mood and a more positive outlook. On the other hand, poor posture can contribute to feelings of discomfort and self-consciousness. For children with autism, who may already face challenges with social interactions and self-esteem, this can be particularly impactful. A slouched or hunched posture might make a child feel more isolated or less engaged in their surroundings, affecting their ability to participate in social activities and build relationships.

The physical impact of poor posture extends beyond just discomfort. It can lead to a range of issues, including back pain, muscular strain, and even difficulties with breathing and digestion. For children with autism, who might be more sensitive to physical discomfort, these issues can be particularly distressing. Chronic pain or discomfort can lead to increased anxiety and agitation, further complicating their emotional and behavioral responses. By encouraging healthy posture, we not only support their physical health but also help to mitigate these additional stressors that can impact their emotional well-being.

Correcting posture involves more than just adjusting how a child sits or stands. It requires a holistic approach that includes developing body awareness and integrating posture into everyday activities. Encouraging a child to engage in activities that promote good posture, such as exercises that strengthen their core muscles and improve their balance, can make a significant difference. Activities like yoga, simple stretching, and even mindful movement can help children become more aware of their bodies and how they move through space. This increased awareness can translate into better posture and, consequently, improved motor skills, sensory processing, and emotional stability.

One effective way to support posture is through regular, gentle reminders and reinforcement. For instance, using visual or tactile cues can help children maintain proper alignment. This might include placing a soft cushion behind them to encourage an upright position or using a visual chart that shows examples of good versus poor posture. Positive reinforcement, such as praise or small rewards, can also encourage children to adopt and maintain healthy posture habits. These strategies can be particularly effective for children who benefit from visual and sensory supports.

It's also important to consider the role of the environment in supporting good posture. Creating a supportive environment involves making sure that the spaces where children spend time, such as their home or classroom, are designed to promote healthy body alignment. This might include adjusting the height of chairs and desks to suit the child's needs, ensuring that seating is comfortable and supportive, and providing opportunities for movement throughout the day. An environment that accommodates and encourages good posture can help children feel more comfortable and supported, which in turn supports their overall development and well-being.

Addressing posture is not just about making adjustments in isolation. It's about understanding how these adjustments fit into the larger picture of a child's development. By integrating posture correction into a broader approach that includes sensory processing, motor development, and emotional support, we create a more comprehensive support system for children with autism. This holistic approach acknowledges the interconnectedness of body and mind, recognizing that improvements in one area can positively influence others.

Ultimately, encouraging healthy posture is a key component of helping children with autism thrive. It's about more than just physical alignment; it's about creating a supportive foundation that enhances their ability to interact with their environment, process sensory information, and feel confident and secure. By focusing on posture, we can make a meaningful difference in their daily lives, offering them greater comfort, improved motor skills, and a more positive emotional state. As we continue to explore strategies for fostering healthy movement patterns, we are not only addressing physical needs but also supporting the broader aspects of their well-being.

Somatic Techniques for Encouraging Healthy Posture

When it comes to fostering healthy posture in children with autism, somatic techniques offer a gentle yet powerful approach. The body is an incredible guide, and by tuning into its signals and responses, we can help children develop better posture and movement patterns that enhance their overall well-being. This process doesn't have to be complex or intimidating. With some simple, easy-toimplement exercises, parents and caregivers can create a supportive environment that encourages their child to maintain a more balanced and functional posture.

One of the foundational principles of somatic therapy is to help individuals become more aware of their bodies and how they move through space. For children with autism, who might struggle with sensory integration or motor coordination, developing an awareness of posture can be incredibly beneficial. An excellent starting point is to introduce exercises that promote body awareness and alignment. One such exercise involves guided body scans. Encourage your child to lie down comfortably on a soft surface, like a yoga mat, and gently guide them through a body scan. Ask them to notice how each part of their body feels against the surface, starting from their feet and moving up to their head. This exercise helps children become more attuned to their body's positioning and encourages them to find a more natural and aligned posture.

Another effective technique is the use of wall exercises, which can be both fun and instructive. Have your child stand with their back against a wall, making sure their heels are a few inches away from the wall. Ask them to gently press their back against the wall while engaging their core muscles. This exercise not only helps them feel the alignment of their spine but also teaches them how to use their core muscles to support their posture. You can make this exercise more engaging by turning it into a game, such as seeing how long they can hold the position or using visual aids like stickers on the wall to help them remember where to place their back.

Incorporating balance exercises can also play a significant role in improving posture. Activities that challenge your child's balance help strengthen their core and improve their overall body awareness. One simple and effective exercise is the balancing beam activity. Place a long, sturdy object like a balance beam or even a line of tape on the floor and encourage your child to walk along it. Start with short distances and gradually increase the length as they gain confidence. This exercise helps them develop better balance and coordination, which are essential for maintaining a healthy posture.

In addition to these exercises, it's important to incorporate movement breaks throughout the day. For children with autism, especially those who may spend extended periods sitting at a desk or in a chair, regular movement breaks can help prevent slouching and encourage a more dynamic posture. Create a routine where your child has scheduled breaks to stretch, move around, or engage in physical activities. For example, you might have a "stretch time" where you guide your child through simple stretching exercises, like reaching for the sky and then bending down to touch their toes. These breaks not only help with posture but also provide valuable sensory input and help regulate their energy levels.

Incorporating playful activities into your posture-promoting routine can also be very effective. Activities like animal walks—where your child imitates the movements of various animals—can be both enjoyable and beneficial. Have them try walking like a bear, crawling like a crab, or hopping like a frog. These movements engage different muscle groups and encourage them to experiment with various body positions, which helps develop a better sense of how their body moves and aligns in space.

Using visual and tactile cues can also support your child in maintaining healthy posture. For instance, you can create a visual chart with pictures or drawings of proper posture and place it in a prominent spot where your child can see it regularly. Additionally, you might use tactile cues such as textured stickers or fabric strips on their chair to remind them to sit up straight or adjust their posture. These cues provide gentle reminders without being intrusive and help reinforce the habit of maintaining a healthy posture.

Integrating proprioceptive activities can further support posture development. Proprioception refers to the body's ability to sense its position and movement in space. Activities that provide deep pressure input, like squeezing a stress ball or using a weighted blanket, can help children become more aware of their body's positioning and promote a sense of stability. These activities can be particularly helpful for children who may struggle with sensory processing challenges, as they provide calming input that supports better posture and body alignment.

Lastly, encourage your child to engage in activities that promote overall physical fitness and strength. Activities like swimming, dancing, or yoga can be particularly beneficial, as they promote flexibility, strength, and coordination. Swimming, for instance, provides full-body exercise and helps improve posture through its focus on body alignment and resistance training. Yoga, on the other hand, offers gentle stretches and poses that enhance body awareness and encourage proper alignment.

By incorporating these somatic techniques into your child's daily routine, you're not just helping them improve their posture—you're also fostering a greater sense of body awareness and emotional well-being. Remember, the goal is to make these exercises enjoyable and engaging, so your child looks forward to them rather than seeing them as a chore. With patience, creativity, and a supportive approach, you can help your child develop and maintain healthy posture, ultimately leading to a more balanced and confident sense of self.

Helping Your Child Build a Stronger Connection Between Mind and Body

Somatic therapy offers a profound way to bridge the gap between the mind and body, especially for children with autism who may struggle with sensory processing and motor coordination. By focusing on the physical sensations and internal experiences of the body, somatic therapy helps to foster a deeper connection between what a child feels and how they move. This strengthened connection is not merely a matter of physical alignment but a holistic approach that touches on emotional, cognitive, and sensory aspects, leading to more intentional and healthy movement patterns.

When children with autism engage in somatic therapy, they start by becoming more aware of their bodily sensations. This awareness is crucial because many children on the spectrum experience difficulty processing sensory information, which can affect their movement patterns and posture. For instance, a child might be unaware of how their body is positioned in space or might struggle to coordinate movements smoothly. Somatic therapy provides a structured yet gentle way to tune into these bodily sensations, which can significantly improve a child's ability to regulate their movements.

One of the key ways somatic therapy fosters this connection is through the practice of mindfulness and body awareness exercises. These exercises encourage children to pay attention to how different parts of their body feel during movement. For example, simple activities like stretching or gentle rocking can help children learn to recognize and respond to the physical signals their bodies are sending. As they become more attuned to these sensations, they develop a better understanding of how their body moves and interacts with its environment. This heightened awareness can lead to improved posture and more coordinated movements, as children learn to adjust their actions based on real-time feedback from their own bodies.

In addition to enhancing awareness, somatic therapy also focuses on teaching children how to move in ways that are both comfortable and efficient. Many children with autism exhibit patterns of movement that may seem unusual or awkward, often due to sensory sensitivities or motor planning difficulties. Through somatic practices, these children can explore and experiment with different ways of moving, gradually finding those that feel more natural and effective. This exploration is supported by exercises that emphasize slow, deliberate movements and body alignment, helping children to build a more solid foundation for their motor skills.

The impact of these practices on a child's posture and motor skills is substantial. Improved body awareness and intentional movement help children develop better control over their posture. For example, a child who learns to recognize when their shoulders are hunched or their back is slumped can make the necessary adjustments to sit or stand with more alignment. This not only improves their overall posture but also reduces physical discomfort and fatigue, which can be particularly important for children who are sensitive to sensory input or who experience discomfort due to poor alignment.

Furthermore, as children with autism develop healthier movement patterns through somatic therapy, they also experience improvements in their motor skills. The therapy helps to refine the coordination between different muscle groups, making movements smoother and more efficient. For instance, activities that involve balancing, reaching, or moving through space encourage the integration of sensory input and motor responses. As children practice these activities, they become more adept at coordinating their movements with their body's sensations, leading to increased proficiency in tasks that require fine and gross motor skills.

Somatic therapy also addresses the emotional and psychological aspects of movement. For many children with autism, anxiety or stress can negatively impact their ability to move comfortably or confidently. By incorporating relaxation techniques and gentle physical touch into therapy, children learn to manage their stress and anxiety more effectively. This not only helps them feel more at ease during movement but also supports their overall well-being. When children feel relaxed and centered, they are more likely to engage in movement with greater ease and fluidity, further enhancing their motor skills and posture.

Another significant benefit of somatic therapy is its ability to promote self-regulation. Through mindful movement practices, children learn to recognize and manage their own physical and emotional states. For example, if a child notices that they are feeling tense or overstimulated, they can use somatic techniques to calm their body and mind before attempting a physical task. This self-regulation supports more intentional and controlled movements, which can lead to improved posture and motor skills over time.

In essence, somatic therapy provides a comprehensive approach to enhancing the mind-body connection, which in turn supports healthier movement patterns and better posture. By helping children with autism become more aware of their bodily sensations, experiment with different movement styles, and manage their stress, this therapy offers valuable tools for developing both physical and emotional resilience. The benefits of somatic therapy extend beyond the immediate improvements in motor skills and posture; they contribute to a greater sense of body awareness and overall well-being, helping children navigate their world with more confidence and ease.

Tracking Progress: Small Adjustments, Big Improvements

When embarking on the journey of improving posture and movement patterns in children with autism, one of the most empowering practices you can adopt is tracking progress. This isn't just about making notes or recording data; it's about understanding and celebrating the small, often subtle changes that, over time, can lead to significant improvements.

Tracking progress is crucial for several reasons. First and foremost, it provides tangible evidence of the effectiveness of the somatic techniques you're implementing. When you start working on posture and movement, it can sometimes feel like progress is slow or even imperceptible. However, keeping track of your child's development helps you see the cumulative effect of the efforts you're making. It helps you recognize that even small adjustments in posture or movement can make a big difference in your child's overall comfort and functional abilities.

Consider this: every small shift in posture or movement, whether it's sitting up a bit straighter or walking with a more balanced gait, contributes to a more significant overall improvement in how your child interacts with their environment. These seemingly minor changes are steps on the path to more significant milestones, like improved coordination, reduced discomfort, and enhanced self-confidence. By tracking these small victories, you can stay motivated and keep your focus on the long-term benefits of your efforts.

One effective way to track progress is through regular observations and documentation. Create a simple chart or journal where you can note any changes you observe in your child's posture or movement patterns. This might include noting how long your child can sit upright at the table, how their balance improves during play, or how their body movements become more fluid and coordinated over time. These records don't have to be extensive or complex—just a few lines a day can make a difference.

Another practical approach is to take photos or videos of your child engaged in various activities. Comparing these over time can provide visual proof of their progress and can be incredibly motivating for both you and your child. Seeing how they've evolved in their posture or movement patterns can be a powerful reminder of the progress they've made. Just remember to approach this with sensitivity and respect for your child's comfort and privacy.

In addition to tracking improvements, celebrating them is equally important. Each small success is a step forward and deserves recognition. This could be as simple as verbal praise, a sticker chart, or a small reward that acknowledges their hard work and persistence. Celebrating these milestones helps reinforce positive behavior and makes the journey more enjoyable for your child. It also builds their confidence, showing them that their efforts are being noticed and valued.

When celebrating progress, it's helpful to focus on the process rather than just the end result. Instead of only praising your child when they achieve a specific goal, also recognize their efforts and dedication. For example, if they're working on sitting with better posture, celebrate their increased ability to stay focused and engaged during activities, even if they haven't yet perfected the posture itself. This approach emphasizes the value of their hard work and perseverance, encouraging them to keep trying and improving.

It's also valuable to involve your child in the tracking and celebrating process. Depending on their age and abilities, you can engage them in setting their own goals and monitoring their progress. This can be empowering for them, as it gives them a sense of ownership over their development. You might use visual aids like charts or stickers to make this process engaging and fun. When they see their progress visually represented, it can be incredibly motivating and affirming.

Moreover, tracking progress isn't just about monitoring improvements—it also helps you identify patterns or areas where your child might be struggling. If you notice that certain movements or postures are consistently challenging for them, you can adjust your approach or seek additional support. This can help you tailor your strategies to better meet your child's needs and ensure that your efforts are as effective as possible.

As you track and celebrate progress, it's important to keep in mind that improvement is often incremental. It's natural for there to be ups and downs along the way. Some days will show more noticeable progress than others, and that's perfectly okay. The key is to stay patient and persistent, focusing on the overall trajectory of improvement rather than getting discouraged by occasional setbacks.

Remember, the journey toward healthier posture and movement patterns is a collaborative one. Your child is an active participant in this process, and your encouragement and support play a crucial role in their success. By tracking progress and celebrating each step forward, you're not just working on improving their physical abilities—you're also fostering a positive and supportive environment that helps them feel valued and motivated.

In summary, tracking progress when working on posture and movement with children is a powerful tool that provides insight, motivation, and a sense of accomplishment. It allows you to witness and celebrate the small victories that lead to significant improvements over time. By adopting a patient, supportive approach and recognizing each step forward, you create a nurturing environment where your child can thrive and develop their full potential.

Part 4

Creating a Supportive Environment for Somatic Therapy

Chapter 7

Setting the Stage for Somatic Therapy at Home

Creating a peaceful, sensory-friendly environment at home is essential for setting the stage for effective somatic therapy, especially for children with autism. The home can become a sanctuary where the body-based practices of somatic therapy are most effective, and crafting this space with care can significantly enhance the therapeutic experience. By focusing on how to organize the space, manage sensory stimuli, and ensure comfort, you can create an environment that not only supports but also nurtures your child's journey through somatic therapy.

The first step in crafting this supportive environment is to consider the organization of the space. Start by designating a specific area in your home where somatic therapy can take place. This doesn't need to be a large or elaborate space; rather, it should be a corner or room that can be consistently used for therapy sessions. Having a dedicated area helps create a sense of routine and predictability, which can be comforting for children on the autism spectrum. In this space, try to keep things uncluttered. A tidy environment can reduce distractions and help your child focus better on the therapeutic activities. Use storage solutions to keep therapy tools, toys, and equipment organized and out of sight when they're not in use. This not only helps maintain a sense of order but also ensures that the space remains inviting and calm.

When it comes to controlling sensory stimuli, it's crucial to tailor the environment to your child's specific sensory needs. For some children, bright lights, loud noises, or strong smells can be overwhelming and counterproductive to therapy. To manage this, consider using soft, natural lighting in the therapy area. Dimmer switches or lamps with adjustable light levels can create a soothing atmosphere. If your child is sensitive to noise, you might invest in noise-canceling headphones or use white noise machines to help mask any disruptive sounds. Additionally, be mindful of any strong odors that could interfere with your child's comfort. Opt for unscented or mildly scented cleaning products and avoid heavily perfumed items in the therapy space.

Creating a calming environment involves more than just controlling sensory input; it also means making the space physically comfortable. Start by ensuring that the space is ergonomically friendly. Invest in comfortable mats or cushions for your child to sit or lie on during therapy sessions. Soft, tactile surfaces can provide a sense of security and support. Bean bags or low, plush seating can also offer a cozy place for your child to relax before or after their sessions. Consider the temperature of the room as well. A space that is too hot or too cold can be distracting, so aim for a comfortable, consistent temperature that suits your child's preferences.

In addition to physical comfort, creating a sensory-friendly environment involves integrating elements that promote relaxation and emotional well-being. Soft, calming colors on the walls and in the décor can contribute to a serene atmosphere. Shades of blue, green, or pastel tones are often soothing and can help reduce anxiety. You might also incorporate elements of nature, such as plants or images of nature, which can have a calming effect. If your child finds comfort in certain textures or items, like a favorite blanket or stuffed animal, make sure these are included in the therapy space. Familiar and comforting objects can provide a sense of stability and reassurance.

It's also beneficial to have a variety of sensory tools available in the therapy area, but be thoughtful about their placement and use. Items like fidget toys, textured balls, or sensory brushes can be wonderful additions, but they should be introduced in a way that doesn't overwhelm your child. Offer these tools during therapy sessions as needed, but avoid cluttering the space with too many items at once. Instead, rotate the tools based on what your child responds to best. This keeps the environment dynamic and engaging without being overwhelming.

Establishing a routine around the therapy space can also be very helpful. Consistency provides a sense of security and can help your child transition into therapy sessions more smoothly. Create a simple routine that your child can anticipate, such as a specific sequence of activities or a particular time of day for therapy. Visual schedules or cues can be helpful in signaling the start of a therapy session, and incorporating calming rituals, like a deep breathing exercise or a favorite calming song, can further ease the transition.

Communication is key when it comes to making the therapy space work for your child. Engage with them to understand their preferences and sensitivities.

Observe their reactions to different elements of the space and be willing to make adjustments based on their feedback. For instance, if your child is particularly sensitive to certain textures, you might need to find alternative materials that feel more comfortable to them. Flexibility and responsiveness to your child's needs will help create a space that is genuinely supportive of their therapy.

Finally, remember that the therapy space should be a place of positive reinforcement and encouragement. Create an atmosphere where your child feels safe and valued. Use this space not only for therapy but also as a haven where your child can experience moments of peace and relaxation. Positive experiences in the therapy space will reinforce their connection to the practices and help build a sense of trust and comfort with the somatic therapy process.

By thoughtfully organizing the space, managing sensory inputs, ensuring physical comfort, and incorporating calming elements, you create an environment that is conducive to effective somatic therapy. This space becomes more than just a room—it transforms into a nurturing retreat that supports your child's emotional and physical well-being. With a well-prepared environment, you provide the foundation for successful therapy sessions and help your child make meaningful progress on their journey.

The Importance of Routine: Establishing Consistency for Best Results

When embarking on the journey of somatic therapy for children with autism, one of the most crucial elements to consider is the role of routine. Establishing a consistent, predictable routine is not just a matter of convenience; it is foundational to the success of therapy. For children with autism, who often thrive on structure and predictability, routine can provide a sense of security and stability that is essential for effective learning and emotional regulation. This consistency helps them feel more comfortable and confident, making it easier for them to engage with the therapeutic practices and integrate them into their daily lives.

Routine in somatic therapy offers a structured framework within which children can explore and understand their bodies and emotions. It creates a predictable environment that helps them anticipate what comes next, reducing anxiety and resistance. When somatic therapy becomes a regular part of their daily or weekly schedule, it transforms from an occasional activity into a meaningful and expected part of their lives. This regularity helps to solidify the benefits of the therapy, as the body and mind become accustomed to the practices and begin to respond more effectively over time.

Consistency in routine is particularly important because it allows children to build and reinforce positive habits. For many children with autism, maintaining new behaviors or techniques can be challenging without the anchor of routine. By embedding somatic therapy into a structured schedule, you provide a consistent opportunity for practice and reinforcement. This repeated exposure helps to solidify the neural pathways involved in the new behaviors or sensations, making them more natural and integrated over time.

Creating a daily or weekly therapy routine that is both structured and flexible can be a balancing act. On one hand, a structured routine provides the predictability that helps children feel secure and focused. On the other hand, flexibility ensures that the routine can be adapted to the child's changing needs and preferences. Striking this balance involves careful planning and a willingness to adjust as needed.

To begin, start by identifying the times of day that work best for incorporating somatic therapy. For some children, early morning sessions might be ideal, setting a positive tone for the day. For others, late afternoon or early evening might be more effective, providing a calming transition from school or other activities. Pay attention to your child's natural rhythms and energy levels, and choose a time when they are most receptive to the therapy.

Once you have identified the optimal times, create a clear and consistent schedule. This could be as simple as setting aside 15-30 minutes each day or a few times a week dedicated to somatic therapy. Make sure to stick to this schedule as closely as possible, as the regularity will help your child become accustomed to the routine. Use visual schedules or timers to help your child understand and anticipate when the therapy will occur, making the routine more concrete and less abstract.

Incorporating somatic therapy into daily life can also be enhanced by integrating it with other routines and activities. For instance, you might include a few minutes of somatic exercises as part of the morning routine before school or as a calming activity before bedtime. By linking the therapy to existing routines, you help reinforce its importance and make it a seamless part of your child's day.

Flexibility is key in ensuring that the routine remains effective and accommodating. Children's needs and preferences can change, and what works one week may need to be adjusted the next. Be prepared to adapt the routine based on your child's responses and feedback. If you notice that a particular time of day or type of activity isn't working as well as expected, don't be afraid to make adjustments. Flexibility also means being open to occasional breaks or modifications, especially during times of increased stress or significant changes in the child's life.

To enhance the effectiveness of the routine, create a supportive and engaging environment. This means setting up a designated space for somatic therapy that is calming and inviting. Choose a quiet, comfortable area where your child can focus on the therapy without distractions. Incorporate elements that make the space enjoyable, such as soft lighting, soothing colors, and calming music. Making the environment pleasant can help your child look forward to the sessions and feel more relaxed during the therapy.

In addition to the physical environment, incorporate positive reinforcement and rewards to make the routine more appealing. Celebrate your child's efforts and progress, no matter how small. This encouragement can motivate them to engage with the therapy more consistently and positively. Over time, as the routine becomes more familiar and integrated into their daily life, the need for external rewards may diminish, and the therapy itself will become its own source of satisfaction and well-being.

Maintaining open communication with your child about the routine is also essential. Even young children can benefit from understanding why the therapy is part of their daily or weekly schedule and how it helps them feel better. Use simple, positive language to explain the purpose of the somatic exercises and involve them in the process as much as possible. This sense of ownership and understanding can make the routine more meaningful and engaging for them.

By combining structure with flexibility, you create a routine that respects your child's need for predictability while allowing room for individualization and adaptation. This approach not only supports the effectiveness of somatic therapy but also helps to build a strong foundation for your child's overall emotional and physical well-being. Through thoughtful planning and a responsive approach, you'll set the stage for a therapeutic routine that nurtures your child's growth and fosters a sense of security and calm in their daily life.

Incorporating Somatic Practices into Everyday Life

Integrating somatic practices into everyday activities is a powerful way to help children with autism connect with their bodies and manage their sensory experiences. It's not about overhauling your daily routine but rather about weaving gentle, mindful movements into the fabric of daily life. This approach can make somatic therapy feel natural and accessible, turning ordinary moments into opportunities for growth and calm.

Consider how playtime can be a rich opportunity for somatic practice. Instead of setting aside special times for therapy, why not infuse these practices into the games and activities your child already enjoys? For example, if your child loves building with blocks, you might incorporate gentle stretching exercises as part of the play. As they reach for the top block, encourage them to stretch their arms up high and then gently roll their shoulders back. This simple movement helps increase body awareness and promotes relaxation. Another idea is to use textured play materials, like playdough or sand, to encourage sensory exploration and fine motor skills. Encourage your child to knead, squish, or mold the material, which not only enhances their tactile sensitivity but also provides calming sensory input.

Meal times also offer a subtle yet effective way to integrate somatic practices. Creating a calming environment at the dining table can help your child feel more settled and focused. Before beginning the meal, guide your child through a brief, mindful breathing exercise. This could be as simple as taking three deep breaths together, inhaling through the nose and exhaling through the mouth, to help ground and center them. You might also encourage slow, deliberate movements during mealtime. For example, as they pick up a spoon or fork, gently remind them to move slowly and mindfully. This not only aids in motor coordination but also helps them stay engaged with the sensory experience of eating.

Bedtime routines are another ideal time to incorporate somatic practices, setting the stage for a peaceful night's sleep. One soothing practice is a bedtime stretch routine. You might guide your child through simple, calming stretches like reaching for the stars, gently rolling their head from side to side, or stretching their legs. These movements can help release any tension accumulated throughout the day and prepare their body for restful sleep. Another technique is to incorporate gentle, rhythmic rocking or swaying motions, either by rocking in a chair or by swaying gently with your child in your arms. This can be particularly calming and help signal to their body that it's time to wind down.

In addition to these specific times, consider how to build somatic awareness into your child's daily routines in more subtle ways. For example, when your child is getting dressed, encourage them to notice the feeling of the fabric against their skin. Ask them to describe the sensation and help them identify which clothes feel most comfortable. This not only builds their sensory awareness but also empowers them to make choices that feel right for them. Similarly, during bath time, incorporate gentle movements and tactile exploration. Let your child feel the water flow through their fingers or use a soft washcloth to explore different textures on their skin.

It's also helpful to create a dedicated space at home where somatic practices can take place. This doesn't need to be a separate room but could be a cozy corner with soft pillows, textured blankets, or a calming sensory tent. This space can serve as a retreat for your child when they need a moment of calm or a place to engage in somatic exercises. By making this space inviting and associated with relaxation, you provide a safe haven where your child can connect with their body and manage sensory input in a supportive environment.

Another key aspect of integrating somatic practices is consistency and patience. It's important to introduce these practices gradually and to be responsive to your child's cues. If they seem hesitant or uncomfortable with a particular exercise, it's okay to adapt or try a different approach. The goal is to create a positive, supportive experience that feels natural rather than forced. Celebrate the small successes and be patient with the process, understanding that building body awareness and sensory regulation takes time.

Finally, involve your child in the process as much as possible. Let them have a say in which activities or practices they enjoy and want to include in their daily routine. This can help them feel more invested and engaged in the somatic practices, making them more likely to participate willingly. For example, if your child enjoys a particular type of movement or sensory activity, encourage them to incorporate that into their daily routine. This personal involvement not only makes the practices more enjoyable but also reinforces their sense of agency and control over their sensory experiences.

Integrating somatic practices into everyday activities doesn't require grand gestures or extensive changes. By embedding mindful movements and sensory exploration into routine moments—whether during play, mealtime, or bedtime—you create a nurturing environment where somatic therapy becomes a natural and supportive part of your child's daily life. This approach helps your child develop greater body awareness, emotional regulation, and overall well-being in a way that feels seamless and authentic.

Tools and Props: Using Simple Items to Enhance Therapy Sessions

Creating a supportive and effective environment for somatic therapy at home doesn't require a lot of fancy equipment or specialized tools. In fact, some of the simplest items can make a world of difference. Let's explore how everyday tools and props like yoga mats, therapy balls, and weighted blankets can enhance your somatic therapy sessions, turning your home into a haven of comfort and healing.

Imagine starting your somatic therapy session with a yoga mat spread out on the floor. This unassuming mat isn't just for yoga; it's a versatile foundation for many somatic practices. Yoga mats provide a cushioned surface that can make movements and stretches more comfortable, particularly for children who might be sensitive to hard or uneven floors. They create a defined space that signals to your child that it's time to focus on their body and sensations. This can be especially helpful if your child is easily distracted or if you're introducing new activities. You can find yoga mats at most sporting goods stores, online retailers, or even discount stores. Look for mats with good grip and thickness to ensure they're both comfortable and safe.

Next, let's talk about therapy balls, often referred to as stability or exercise balls. These large, inflatable balls are fantastic for engaging your child's core muscles, improving balance, and enhancing body awareness. Sitting on a therapy ball can help children with autism develop better posture and coordination. It's also a fun way to introduce movement that doesn't feel like traditional exercise. Therapy balls come in various sizes, so choose one that's appropriate for your child's height. You can purchase them from specialized therapy supply stores, online retailers, or even large department stores with a sports section. When using therapy balls, make sure the surface is stable and that there's enough room around the ball to move safely. You might also want to have your child try different activities on the ball, such as gentle bouncing, rolling, or simply sitting and engaging in activities like drawing or playing games.

Weighted blankets are another tool that can make a big impact in somatic therapy. These blankets, filled with materials like glass beads or plastic pellets, provide gentle, even pressure that can help soothe a child's nervous system. The deep touch pressure from a weighted blanket can be particularly comforting for children with sensory processing challenges, helping them feel more grounded and secure. To incorporate a weighted blanket into your somatic therapy sessions, consider using it during relaxation exercises or while your child is engaging in quiet activities. It can also be a comforting addition to a bedtime routine, helping your child transition more smoothly to sleep. Weighted blankets are available from various retailers, including online specialty stores, bedding stores, and even some major department stores. When choosing a weighted blanket, it's important to select one that is appropriately weighted for your child's size and weight, usually around 10% of their body weight.

Beyond these specific tools, creating a calming and inviting therapy space is crucial. This might involve setting up a cozy corner with soft lighting, calming colors, and perhaps some soothing music. A space that feels welcoming can help your child feel more at ease and open to the therapeutic process. Consider adding elements like a soft rug or bean bags where your child can comfortably sit or lie down. These small touches can make the therapy space feel less clinical and more like a nurturing environment.

Using these tools effectively involves more than just having them on hand—it's about incorporating them thoughtfully into your sessions. For instance, if you're introducing a new tool like a therapy ball or weighted blanket, start with short, positive experiences. Gradually increase the time and variety of activities as your child becomes more comfortable. It's also important to observe your child's responses to different tools. If they seem overwhelmed or disinterested, it might be helpful to adjust the approach or try a different tool. Remember, the goal is to support your child's unique needs and preferences, not to adhere to a rigid protocol.

Another tip is to involve your child in setting up the therapy space. Allowing them to choose their favorite mat color or pick out a therapy ball that appeals to them can make the process feel more personal and engaging. This can also help them feel a greater sense of ownership and comfort with the tools they're using.

As you incorporate these tools into your home therapy sessions, keep in mind that consistency and patience are key. It may take some time for your child to adapt to new practices or to see the full benefits of the tools you're using. Approach each session with a sense of curiosity and flexibility, adjusting as needed based on your child's responses and progress.

The beauty of using simple tools and props in somatic therapy is that they don't have to be elaborate or expensive to be effective. With a little creativity and attentiveness, you can turn everyday items into powerful aids in your child's therapeutic journey. By creating a supportive environment and using these tools thoughtfully, you're not just enhancing your child's therapy sessions—you're fostering a sense of comfort and connection that can have a lasting positive impact on their well-being.

Chapter 8

Working with Therapists and Other Professionals

Finding the right somatic therapist for a child with autism can be a transformative step toward enhancing their emotional well-being and sensory regulation. This journey often starts with understanding what to look for in a therapist who specializes in working with children with autism. It's not just about finding someone with the right qualifications; it's about finding a compassionate partner who truly understands your child's unique needs and can offer a nurturing, effective therapeutic experience.

When searching for a somatic therapist, qualifications are undeniably important, but they are just one part of a much broader picture. Start by ensuring that the therapist has formal training in somatic therapy. This could mean a background in body-based approaches like Sensorimotor Psychotherapy, Somatic Experiencing, or other modalities specifically designed to address bodily experiences and responses. Look for certifications or degrees in these areas, as they indicate a solid foundation in the principles of somatic therapy.

However, qualifications alone don't guarantee that a therapist will be a good fit for your child. Experience, particularly with children on the autism spectrum, plays a crucial role. Somatic therapy with children requires not only an understanding of somatic principles but also a nuanced approach to working with neurodivergent children. Seek out therapists who have a proven track record of working with autistic children. This experience is invaluable because it means they are familiar with the sensory and emotional challenges that these children face and are adept at adapting their techniques to meet those needs.

Another key aspect to consider is the therapist's approach and how it aligns with your child's needs. Somatic therapy can encompass a range of techniques and philosophies, from gentle touch and movement to more active engagement with the child's bodily sensations. It's important to find a therapist whose approach resonates with your child's comfort levels and therapeutic goals. Some children might benefit from a therapist who integrates play and movement into their sessions, while others may respond better to a more structured approach. During initial consultations, discuss the therapist's methods and observe how they interact with your child. This interaction can provide insights into their style and effectiveness.

Equally important is the therapist's ability to build a strong, trusting relationship with your child. Somatic therapy is inherently personal and relies on the child's ability to feel safe and understood. Look for signs that the therapist is genuinely empathetic and patient, someone who takes the time to understand your child's unique experiences and challenges. They should be able to communicate with sensitivity and respect, making your child feel comfortable and secure.

In addition to their professional skills and experience, consider how well the therapist communicates and collaborates with you as a parent. Effective therapy often involves a partnership between the therapist and the family. The therapist should be open to discussing treatment goals, progress, and any concerns you might have. They should also be willing to provide you with strategies and exercises to support your child's progress at home. This collaborative approach ensures that therapy extends beyond the session, integrating into your child's daily life.

Finding the right somatic therapist also involves practical considerations. Ensure that the therapist is conveniently located and that their availability fits with your family's schedule. Sometimes, the best-qualified therapist might not be practical due to logistical issues. It's important to find someone whose sessions you can attend consistently, as continuity is key in therapy. Additionally, check if the therapist's fees are covered by your insurance or if they offer a sliding scale. Financial considerations can be a significant factor in the long-term success of therapy.

Don't hesitate to seek recommendations from other parents, professionals, or support groups. Word-of-mouth referrals can provide valuable insights into a therapist's effectiveness and approach. Sometimes, personal experiences shared by others can help you find a therapist who is both highly skilled and highly recommended by those who understand your child's specific needs.

As you embark on this search, trust your instincts as a parent. You know your child better than anyone else. Pay attention to how your child responds to potential therapists and whether they seem comfortable and engaged. A positive, trusting relationship with the therapist is crucial for effective therapy, so ensure that your child feels at ease with their new therapist.

In your quest for the right somatic therapist, remember that this process might take time. It's a journey of exploration and finding the best fit for your child's unique needs. Be patient and open to adjusting your approach if necessary. The goal is to find a therapist who not only has the right credentials but also connects with your child in a meaningful way.

Ultimately, the right somatic therapist will be someone who combines professional expertise with a deep understanding of your child's individual experiences. They will work collaboratively with you to create a supportive, effective therapeutic environment that helps your child navigate their sensory and emotional world. This partnership is a crucial step in your child's path to greater emotional well-being and comfort in their own body.

Collaborating with Your Child's Therapist for Optimal Results

Collaboration between parents and therapists is the cornerstone of effective somatic therapy for children with autism. This partnership isn't just beneficial—it's essential for achieving the best outcomes. When parents and therapists work together, they create a cohesive support system that can more accurately address a child's unique needs, celebrate their progress, and navigate any challenges that arise along the way.

Imagine the journey of somatic therapy as a collaborative dance between home and therapy sessions. The therapist brings their expertise in body-based practices, guiding the child through techniques designed to improve emotional regulation, sensory processing, and motor skills. Meanwhile, parents are the constant presence in the child's life, providing context, continuity, and encouragement. When both parties are in sync, the therapy process becomes a seamless extension of the child's everyday experiences rather than a series of isolated events.

Effective communication is the linchpin of this collaboration. Parents should feel empowered to share their observations and concerns with the therapist, providing valuable insights into their child's reactions and progress outside the therapy room. This exchange of information helps the therapist tailor their approach, ensuring that the techniques and goals are relevant and responsive to the child's evolving needs. Conversely, therapists can offer parents guidance on how to reinforce the practices at home, suggest adjustments to daily routines, and provide feedback on how the child is adapting to the therapy.

Regular check-ins and progress reviews are another critical component of successful collaboration. These meetings are opportunities for parents and therapists to discuss the child's development, celebrate successes, and identify areas that might need further attention. It's important for parents to be proactive during these discussions, asking questions about the therapy's effectiveness, understanding the goals being set, and seeking advice on how to support their child's progress. This ongoing dialogue ensures that everyone is aligned and working towards the same objectives, making it easier to adjust strategies as needed.

Creating a shared vision for the child's therapy goals is also crucial. Both parents and therapists should have a clear understanding of what they hope to achieve through somatic therapy. This shared vision helps to set realistic and meaningful goals that reflect the child's individual needs and abilities. By setting these goals together, parents and therapists can work in harmony to track progress and make informed decisions about next steps. This collaboration fosters a sense of teamwork and mutual investment in the child's success.

Additionally, parents can play a proactive role by integrating somatic practices into their child's daily life. The therapist might introduce specific exercises or techniques during sessions, but it's often the daily, consistent reinforcement at home that solidifies these practices. Parents can create a supportive environment that encourages the child to engage with these techniques regularly, thus enhancing their effectiveness. It's through this daily reinforcement that the benefits of somatic therapy truly begin to take root, helping the child to build resilience and self-awareness over time.

Lastly, celebrating milestones, no matter how small, can strengthen the partnership between parents and therapists. Acknowledging these achievements not only motivates the child but also reinforces the collaborative efforts of everyone involved. It's a reminder that progress is a shared success and that every step forward is a testament to the collective dedication of parents and therapists working together.

In essence, the relationship between parents and therapists is a dynamic, evolving partnership that is central to the success of somatic therapy. By maintaining open lines of communication, setting shared goals, and actively participating in the therapy process, both parties can create a supportive framework that fosters the child's growth and well-being. This collaborative approach ensures that somatic therapy is not just a series of therapeutic interventions but a meaningful journey of connection, progress, and shared achievement.

The Role of Other Professionals: Integrating Somatic Therapy with OT, PT, and More

Integrating somatic therapy with other therapeutic modalities, such as occupational therapy (OT) and physical therapy (PT), opens up a world of possibilities for supporting children with autism. When we talk about a multidisciplinary approach, we're not just adding different therapies into the mix—we're creating a collaborative symphony where each modality enhances and supports the others, working towards a common goal of holistic, individualized care.

Somatic therapy, with its focus on body awareness and sensory processing, can beautifully complement occupational therapy. OT often concentrates on helping children develop daily living skills, fine motor skills, and sensory integration. For a child with autism, these goals are critical, yet they often face unique sensory challenges and difficulties with motor planning and coordination. This is where somatic therapy can step in, offering a deeper layer of support. Through techniques such as mindful movement and body awareness exercises, somatic therapy helps children become more attuned to their bodies. This increased body awareness can make OT activities more accessible and effective. For instance, if a child struggles with proprioception—the sense of their body's position in space—somatic exercises can help them develop a clearer understanding of their bodily movements, which can make tasks like buttoning a shirt or using utensils less overwhelming.

Moreover, somatic therapy's emphasis on emotional regulation can also dovetail with OT's focus on sensory processing. Many children with autism experience sensory overload or have difficulty modulating their sensory responses. By integrating somatic practices that promote relaxation and grounding, we can help these children manage sensory input more effectively. This, in turn, can make OT sessions more productive, as the child's ability to process sensory information improves. For example, a child who has learned to use deep breathing techniques from somatic therapy might find it easier to participate in an OT activity that involves sensory exploration, such as playing with textured materials or engaging in fine motor tasks.

Similarly, somatic therapy can be a valuable ally to physical therapy. PT aims to improve physical function and mobility, often through exercises that enhance strength, balance, and coordination. Children with autism frequently encounter motor challenges that PT addresses, but these challenges are often intertwined with sensory and emotional factors. Somatic therapy can help bridge this gap by focusing on how the body feels and moves, not just on the mechanics of movement. Through techniques like gentle stretching, sensory awareness exercises, and proprioceptive activities, somatic therapy can support PT goals by helping children become more aware of their physical sensations and movements. This heightened body awareness can lead to improved coordination and balance, making PT exercises more effective and enjoyable for the child.

The benefits of a multidisciplinary approach extend beyond the individual therapies themselves. When therapists from different disciplines collaborate, they can create a more cohesive and tailored plan of care. For instance, an OT and PT working together can align their goals and strategies, ensuring that their interventions complement each other and address the child's needs comprehensively. If OT focuses on fine motor skills, while PT addresses gross motor skills, somatic therapy can tie these efforts together by enhancing overall body awareness and emotional readiness. This integrated approach ensures that all aspects of the child's development are addressed in a harmonious and supportive manner.

Collaboration between professionals also fosters a more holistic understanding of the child's needs. Each therapist brings a unique perspective and expertise, and when these perspectives are shared and integrated, they provide a richer, more complete view of the child's strengths and challenges. This collaborative approach allows for more informed decision-making and personalized care plans. For example, if a child's sensory processing issues are affecting both their fine and gross motor skills, a team approach can address these issues from multiple angles, using strategies from OT, PT, and somatic therapy to provide comprehensive support.

Communication is key in this multidisciplinary framework. Regular meetings and open lines of communication between therapists ensure that everyone involved is on the same page regarding the child's progress, goals, and challenges. This ongoing dialogue helps to adjust and refine therapeutic approaches as needed, ensuring that interventions remain relevant and effective. For example, if a child is making strides in somatic therapy but is still struggling with specific OT or PT tasks, therapists can work together to adjust their strategies or introduce new techniques that build on the child's progress.

Parents and caregivers also play a crucial role in this collaborative process. They offer valuable insights into their child's daily experiences, preferences, and responses to different therapies. By working closely with therapists, parents can help to ensure that the therapeutic interventions are aligned with the child's needs and goals. Additionally, therapists can provide parents with practical strategies and activities to reinforce therapy goals at home, creating a consistent support system that extends beyond the therapy sessions.

It's important to recognize that each child is unique, and what works for one may not work for another. A multidisciplinary approach allows for flexibility and creativity in finding the best ways to support each child's individual needs. By combining the strengths of somatic therapy with those of OT and PT, we can create a more comprehensive and supportive therapeutic experience that addresses not just the physical aspects of development, but also the emotional and sensory dimensions.

In essence, the integration of somatic therapy with other therapeutic approaches exemplifies the power of collaboration in supporting children with autism. It's about more than just combining techniques; it's about creating a cohesive and responsive plan of care that recognizes and nurtures the whole child. When therapists work together, drawing on their diverse expertise and perspectives, they create a richer, more supportive environment that helps children thrive.

Through this collaborative approach, we can offer children with autism the best possible chance to develop their full potential, finding greater ease, confidence, and joy in their daily lives.

Communicating with Teachers and Schools to Support Somatic Practices

Navigating the school environment can sometimes feel like a maze, especially when you're trying to integrate somatic therapy practices into your child's daily routine. But don't worry—you're not alone in this, and with a bit of planning and communication, you can ensure that your child's needs are understood and supported by their teachers and school staff. Here's how to make that process smoother and more effective:

First things first, when approaching teachers and school staff about somatic therapy, think of it as starting a conversation with a partner who's there to support your child's success. Begin by sharing what somatic therapy is and how it benefits your child. It's often helpful to explain it in simple, relatable terms. For example, you might say, "Somatic therapy helps my child feel more grounded and calm by focusing on body movements and breathing exercises. These techniques have really helped at home, and I'd love to explore how they might be integrated into their school day."

Being clear about the benefits is key. Emphasize how somatic techniques can help manage anxiety, improve focus, and support emotional regulation. You could explain, "These exercises can help my child stay focused and manage stress better, which might make it easier for them to engage in classroom activities and interactions."

Next, offer specific suggestions for incorporating somatic techniques into the classroom environment. For instance, you might suggest brief, calming exercises that can be done at the start of the day or before transitioning between subjects. A simple breathing exercise or a quick stretch can be incredibly effective in helping children reset their focus and energy. You could propose, "It might be helpful to start the day with a short breathing exercise or a few minutes of stretching to help my child feel more centered and ready to learn."

Encourage teachers to observe how your child responds to these techniques and be open to feedback. This approach can foster a collaborative atmosphere where adjustments can be made based on what works best in the classroom setting. You might say, "I'd appreciate your observations on how my child responds to these techniques. We can adjust as needed to find what works best for them."

Be prepared to provide some resources or training materials about somatic practices. Offering to share information or even a brief training session on the basics can help teachers feel more confident in using these techniques. For example, "I can provide some materials that explain the exercises we use, and if you're interested, I'd be happy to do a brief training on how to incorporate them into your routine."

Maintaining open and ongoing communication is crucial. Schedule regular check-ins with teachers to discuss your child's progress and any adjustments that might be needed. These conversations can be a great opportunity to share successes and address any challenges. You might arrange, "Let's schedule a time to discuss how things are going and any adjustments we might need to make. I'm here to support you in any way I can."

Finally, celebrate the efforts of the teachers and school staff in supporting your child. Positive reinforcement can go a long way in building a strong partnership. A simple note of thanks or an acknowledgment of their efforts can make a big difference. You might say, "I really appreciate your efforts in helping my child integrate these techniques. Your support means a lot to us."

By approaching the conversation with clarity, openness, and collaboration, you'll help ensure that your child's somatic therapy practices are understood and supported in the school environment. Together, you can create a more harmonious and supportive learning experience that aligns with your child's needs and promotes their overall well-being.

Part 5

Progress and Growth: What to Expect on This Journey

Chapter 9

Tracking Your Child's Progress: Small Wins and Big Milestones

When your child begins their journey with somatic therapy, it's natural to want to see immediate, dramatic changes. After all, you're investing time and energy into this process with the hope that it will make a significant difference in their emotional and physical well-being. However, one of the most important things to remember about somatic therapy is that the progress can often be subtle, especially at first. It's less about grand transformations and more about noticing the small, quiet shifts that build over time into something much larger. These subtle signs of progress are incredibly meaningful and are worth celebrating as they indicate that your child's body and mind are slowly recalibrating, finding balance, and becoming more aligned.

One of the first and most common indicators of progress in somatic therapy is improved emotional regulation. Children on the autism spectrum often struggle with managing overwhelming emotions like anxiety, frustration, or anger. This can lead to frequent meltdowns or shutdowns, leaving both the child and the parent feeling exhausted. However, through somatic therapy, children gradually learn to connect with their body's sensations, which can help them become more aware of their emotional states. A small but significant shift might be noticing that your child is able to calm themselves down a little quicker than before. Perhaps they still get upset when they're overstimulated, but instead of melting down for an hour, they recover in thirty minutes. These are the kinds of wins that may seem small on the surface, but they signal that your child is learning how to regulate their nervous system more effectively.

As your child continues their somatic therapy journey, you may also notice improvements in their ability to communicate their feelings, even if it's nonverbal. Maybe they're able to use a gesture or a sound to let you know they're feeling overwhelmed before they reach a breaking point. This kind of self-awareness is huge, and while it may not seem like a big milestone compared to traditional developmental markers, it's an essential skill for children on the spectrum. Somatic therapy teaches them to listen to their body's cues, and as they grow more attuned to these signals, they can communicate their needs with greater clarity. It might be as simple as your child taking a deep breath when they're stressed or choosing to step away from a noisy environment before it becomes too much to handle. These are the kinds of small wins that indicate real progress.

Another subtle sign of growth you may observe is better posture. It sounds almost too simple to be significant, but posture is deeply connected to a person's sense of well-being and how they move through the world. Many children on the autism spectrum have postural challenges due to muscle tension, poor motor coordination, or sensory sensitivities. Somatic therapy helps children become more aware of how they hold their body and encourages them to release tension and find a more natural, aligned posture. Over time, you might notice that your child stands or sits with a bit more ease. Their shoulders might not be hunched up by their ears as much, or they might walk with a little more balance. These changes are subtle but important because when a child feels more comfortable in their body, they're more likely to feel secure and confident in other areas of their life as well.

Reduced sensory sensitivity is another area where parents often see gradual improvements. Sensory overload is a common issue for children on the autism spectrum, and it can lead to heightened anxiety, emotional outbursts, or withdrawal. Through somatic therapy, children learn to recognize the signals their body sends when they're becoming overstimulated, and they can begin to develop strategies to cope. Maybe your child used to cover their ears and scream when they heard a loud noise, but now they simply flinch or seek out a quieter space. Or perhaps they used to refuse certain textures of clothing but have recently become more tolerant of different fabrics. These small shifts might not seem like much, but they indicate that your child's sensory system is becoming more regulated, allowing them to engage with the world in a way that feels safer and less overwhelming.

Another small but profound sign of progress is when a child begins to show greater flexibility in their movements. Many children with autism have difficulty with motor coordination, which can manifest as stiff, awkward, or repetitive movements. Somatic therapy encourages fluidity in movement and helps children become more attuned to how their body moves through space. Over time, you might notice that your child's movements become a bit more graceful or that they seem less rigid when performing everyday tasks. For example, a child who once struggled to tie their shoes due to poor motor control might suddenly master the task, or they might begin to enjoy activities like dancing or swimming, where before they would have avoided them. These small but significant shifts in motor skills are an indication that somatic therapy is helping your child feel more comfortable and capable in their own body.

Emotional resilience is another area where subtle growth can be observed. Children on the autism spectrum often have a harder time bouncing back from difficult situations or changes in routine. A small but meaningful sign of progress in somatic therapy could be noticing that your child is a little more adaptable when plans change. Maybe they no longer have a complete meltdown when their routine is disrupted, or they're able to handle transitions a bit more smoothly. This resilience doesn't develop overnight, but as your child becomes more in tune with their body's signals, they begin to build an inner strength that helps them cope with life's inevitable ups and downs. Even if these moments of adaptability are fleeting, they are important markers of progress.

You may also notice a change in how your child interacts socially. Somatic therapy isn't just about helping children feel more at home in their bodies;

it also has the potential to enhance their relationships with others. For children with autism, social interactions can be challenging due to difficulties with reading social cues, managing emotions, or sensory sensitivities in group settings. But as they develop greater body awareness and emotional regulation, they may begin to feel more comfortable engaging with peers or family members. Maybe your child starts to initiate a hug, or they're able to maintain eye contact for a few seconds longer than before. These moments of connection, no matter how brief, are important signs that your child is feeling more secure in themselves and in their relationships with others.

Sleep patterns can also be an area where parents see subtle progress. Many children on the spectrum struggle with sleep due to heightened sensory awareness or anxiety. Somatic therapy helps to calm the nervous system, and over time, you might notice that your child falls asleep a little more easily or wakes up feeling a bit more rested. These small improvements in sleep can have a ripple effect, enhancing your child's mood, energy levels, and overall well-being. While a full night of uninterrupted sleep may still be a distant goal, any shift toward more restful sleep is a sign that your child's nervous system is beginning to find balance.

As you track your child's progress, it's also important to recognize the shifts in their confidence and self-esteem. Children who feel out of sync with their bodies often struggle with a sense of insecurity or self-doubt. Somatic therapy, by helping them feel more grounded and comfortable in their physical being, can foster a growing sense of confidence. You might notice that your child seems a little more willing to try new things, or that they're more assertive in expressing their needs. These are signs that they're beginning to trust themselves and feel more at ease in their own skin.

Ultimately, the key to recognizing these subtle signs of progress is to remain attuned to the small moments and incremental changes. It's easy to overlook these shifts when you're focused on the bigger picture, but each small win is a stepping stone on your child's journey. Somatic therapy works slowly and gently, creating a foundation for long-term growth and well-being. By paying attention to the small details—whether it's a calmer response to stress, a slight improvement in coordination, or a moment of greater social connection—you'll begin to see just how far your child is coming, even if the progress isn't immediately dramatic. These subtle signs are the foundation for the more visible milestones that will come later, and they are a testament to the resilience, strength, and capacity for growth that your child possesses.

Celebrating Successes—Big and Small

Celebrating every success, no matter how small, is an essential part of a child's somatic therapy journey, especially for children with autism. These children face unique challenges daily, and their progress, whether it's a slight shift in how they move or a deeper moment of emotional regulation, is worth honoring. By acknowledging each step forward, we create an environment where the child feels seen, supported, and empowered to keep trying. The act of celebration doesn't just mark progress; it actively shapes a child's mindset, builds their confidence, and motivates them to continue moving forward.

In somatic therapy, even the smallest achievements can be profound. For example, a child who has difficulty with sensory overload might begin to tolerate different textures or sounds for the first time. To an outsider, this may seem insignificant, but for the child and their family, it's monumental. Recognizing these moments encourages the child to embrace new experiences with less fear. When parents or therapists notice these changes and celebrate them with excitement, it sends the message that effort matters and that progress, no matter how gradual, is valuable. In this way, celebration is not just an acknowledgment of a result but an affirmation of the process, reinforcing the idea that trying is as important as succeeding.

These moments of success, whether they come after days of focused effort or appear seemingly out of nowhere, provide opportunities to build a child's confidence. Confidence in children with autism can sometimes be fragile, especially when they struggle to meet conventional expectations or compare themselves to others. But when a child sees their small wins being noticed and celebrated, they begin to internalize a sense of achievement. Perhaps a child who has difficulty with motor coordination manages to balance on one foot for a few seconds, or maybe they learn to relax their shoulders in moments of tension—both of these can be celebrated as significant steps forward in somatic therapy. Each moment acknowledged helps to build a narrative for the child that says, "I am capable. I can improve. My efforts matter."

Motivation is another key reason why celebrating every success matters. Somatic therapy often requires repetition and patience, and children can easily become discouraged if they don't see the fruits of their labor right away. By celebrating small wins, we create moments of positive reinforcement that can energize the child's desire to keep going. A child who hears, "Look at how much better you are at this than last week!" feels an intrinsic motivation to continue improving. They see that their work is paying off, even if the gains are small. This fuels their engagement with therapy and gives them the stamina to push through the inevitable plateaus or setbacks that are part of any therapeutic journey.

Take, for example, a child learning to regulate their breathing as part of somatic therapy exercises designed to reduce anxiety. In the beginning, this might feel impossible for them—perhaps their breath is shallow, and they are unable to focus on slowing it down. But after weeks of practice, they might have a moment where, without prompting, they take a deep, calming breath in response to a stressful situation. This is a moment worth celebrating. It shows that the body is beginning to internalize the practices, creating new patterns of response that can have a profound impact on the child's daily life. The child may not fully understand the significance of this change, but when it is acknowledged—whether through verbal praise, a high-five, or even just a joyful smile—it reinforces that they are on the right track. The celebration itself becomes a form of positive feedback, making it more likely that the child will continue to engage in the exercises that are helping them grow.

Moreover, celebrating small wins fosters a sense of connection between the child and the adults supporting them. When a therapist or parent takes the time to recognize the child's achievements, it communicates that they are paying attention, that they care, and that they are invested in the child's journey. This can strengthen the bond of trust, making the child feel more comfortable and open during somatic therapy sessions. Trust is critical in this work because many children with autism may initially resist body-based interventions. Their heightened sensitivity or past experiences may make them wary of physical exercises. But when they begin to see that their efforts are met with encouragement and celebration, it creates a positive association with the therapy. The child learns to expect not just challenges but moments of recognition and joy.

Celebration is also a way to counterbalance the focus on what is difficult or lacking. All too often, therapy is about addressing deficits—what the child can't do yet or where they need improvement. While it's important to have goals and work toward them, a constant focus on what is "wrong" can be disheartening. This is where celebrating small wins becomes so crucial. It shifts the narrative from one of deficiency to one of growth. A child might struggle with coordination, but perhaps they showed a little more fluidity today than they did last week. That small improvement is worth celebrating because it reminds the child (and the adults around them) that progress is happening, even if it's not immediately obvious. This shift in perspective can reduce the pressure on the child and create a more positive, nurturing environment for their development.

Consider a child who struggles with grounding themselves after a sensory meltdown. After months of work, they manage to calm themselves more quickly using a grounding technique they learned in somatic therapy. This might seem like a small step when the meltdown still occurred, but it's an important milestone. The ability to recover faster is a sign of growing self-regulation, a skill that will serve them in many aspects of their life. When this moment is celebrated, it reinforces the child's ability to manage their emotional responses. The child begins to see themselves as capable of self-soothing, and this belief fuels further progress.

Finally, celebrating every success, big or small, helps to cultivate a positive emotional environment. Therapy can be hard work, and for many children, particularly those on the autism spectrum, the physical and emotional demands of somatic therapy can feel overwhelming. But when therapy sessions are infused with moments of celebration, they become experiences the child can look forward to. It transforms the process from something they endure into something they actively participate in. This emotional shift is vital because therapy should never feel like a punishment or an endless series of obstacles. It should feel like a journey, one where every step—whether it's a baby step or a leap—gets recognized and honored.

In the end, celebrating each success in somatic therapy helps to nurture a mindset of resilience, positivity, and perseverance. It teaches children with autism that progress doesn't always come in big, dramatic leaps but often in small, quiet moments of growth. By noticing and celebrating these moments, we help them build confidence, stay motivated, and feel supported on their journey.

Keeping a Therapy Journal: Tracking Improvements Over Time

Keeping a therapy journal can be one of the most valuable tools you have as you embark on the journey of helping your child through somatic therapy. It's not just about writing down observations—it's about creating a space where you can capture the subtle shifts in your child's behavior, track emotional changes, and celebrate those small yet meaningful milestones that might otherwise go unnoticed. A journal gives you a way to look back and see progress in a concrete way, offering reassurance during moments when it might feel like you're not moving forward as quickly as you'd hoped.

One of the biggest benefits of keeping a journal is that it helps you stay present and mindful in the process. When you're living in the day-to-day rhythm of parenting, it's easy to miss the small wins—those moments when your child handles a sensory challenge with more ease, or when they seem calmer after an activity. Writing these things down, even if it's just a quick note, allows you to capture the progress as it unfolds, so you can look back later and see the cumulative effect of these seemingly minor changes. Over time, these small wins add up, and a journal allows you to recognize and celebrate them.

A journal also helps you track patterns in your child's behavior. As you begin to record observations about how they respond to different somatic exercises or how their mood changes after a particularly stressful day, you might start to notice trends. Maybe they're more anxious on days when they've been overstimulated, or perhaps certain exercises consistently lead to better sleep. These patterns can be incredibly helpful, not just for you as a parent, but also for any therapists or professionals working with your child. It gives them a richer understanding of what's working and what's not, and it helps everyone involved stay aligned in their approach.

When it comes to what to include in your journal, think of it as a flexible tool that evolves with your needs. Start by noting down the specific behaviors you're observing. These can be anything from how your child reacts to a new sensory experience to their level of focus during a somatic exercise. You might also want to include details about their mood throughout the day. Are they more withdrawn? More open? Tracking these emotional shifts over time can give you insight into how the therapy is impacting their overall well-being.

Another important aspect to document are the milestones—both big and small. This might mean recording when your child first tries a new movement or when they show increased coordination during an activity. It could be something as significant as maintaining eye contact longer than usual or something more subtle, like remaining calm in a situation that would have previously triggered anxiety. These milestones, no matter how minor they may seem, are worth celebrating and acknowledging in your journal. It gives you a sense of forward momentum and reminds you that progress is happening, even if it's at a pace that might not always feel immediate.

Emotional changes are also worth paying attention to. Over time, somatic therapy often leads to shifts in how children process their emotions. Maybe your child is starting to use words to express how they're feeling, or perhaps they're learning to calm themselves down in ways they weren't able to before.

Noting these moments in your journal helps you stay aware of the emotional growth that's taking place alongside the physical changes.

Finally, remember that your journal doesn't have to be perfect. It's not about creating a polished record—it's about capturing the real, raw moments of your child's progress. Some days you might write paragraphs, and other days it might just be a few words. The key is to make it a practice, a way to check in with yourself and your child, and to keep track of the journey you're on together. Over time, you'll find that the journal becomes a cherished part of your experience, offering a source of insight, reflection, and even comfort on days when the progress feels harder to see.

Adapting and Evolving: Adjusting Your Approach as Your Child Grows

As a child with autism grows, their needs, challenges, and strengths evolve. This means that the approach to somatic therapy should not remain static but must adapt to meet these changing needs. Children are not fixed in their development; they move through different stages of growth, both physically and emotionally, and their experience of the world shifts as they gain new skills and face new challenges. What worked at one stage might not be as effective at another. Therefore, it's important for parents and therapists to remain flexible, open to adjusting therapy goals and techniques to match where the child is in their journey.

At the core of this adaptability is an understanding that therapy is not a one-size-fits-all, linear process. When we think of somatic therapy, we often imagine a set of structured exercises aimed at helping a child regulate their sensory experiences, calm their nervous system, and improve motor coordination. But it's more than that. Somatic therapy is deeply intuitive, and it requires the therapist, the child, and the parent to work together as a team, continually responding to the child's changing body and mind.

As a child grows, their body changes. These changes—ranging from physical growth spurts to new motor skills—can affect how they experience the world and how they respond to therapeutic exercises. A child who once needed intense sensory input to feel grounded might reach a point where they're more sensitive to that input and need lighter, more nuanced forms of movement. Similarly, a child who struggled with balance and coordination early on may develop these skills over time, requiring the therapy to shift focus toward more fine motor tasks or social interactions rather than the gross motor work they initially started with.

Adapting to these changes requires ongoing collaboration between parents and therapists. Parents play a crucial role in observing and communicating their child's progress outside of therapy sessions. They are the ones who see the subtle shifts, the small wins that might not always be obvious in a clinical setting. Maybe it's the way their child has begun to tolerate certain textures, or the way they seem more comfortable in their own skin during everyday activities. These observations are valuable because they provide insight into how the child is responding to therapy, and they help guide decisions about how the approach should evolve.

Regular communication between the therapist and the parent is essential to ensure that therapy remains effective and attuned to the child's growth. This isn't just about scheduling check-ins or attending appointments—it's about creating a partnership where the parent feels empowered to voice their concerns, share successes, and collaborate on goal setting. Together, parents and therapists can review the child's developmental progress and adjust the therapeutic approach accordingly.

One of the key aspects of this process is updating therapy goals. As the child makes progress, the goals of therapy should reflect their current capabilities and needs. If a child has mastered certain motor skills or has become more adept at calming themselves when overwhelmed, it might be time to shift focus to other areas where they still need support. For instance, early therapy sessions might have centered around helping the child become more aware of their body and managing sensory overload. As they grow older, the focus might move toward building more complex social interactions or enhancing self-regulation strategies in new environments, like school or social settings.

Therapists can guide parents in understanding how these changing goals align with their child's overall development. For example, if a child has reached a point where they can effectively calm themselves through specific somatic techniques, the therapist might introduce exercises that promote more independence in using those techniques without adult guidance. The goal is to scaffold the child's skills, building on what they've already learned while gradually introducing new challenges that push them to grow.

It's also important to recognize that as children with autism grow older, their emotional needs often become more complex. In early childhood, therapy might focus heavily on managing sensory experiences and regulating the body's response to stimuli. But as children enter adolescence and start to navigate more social and emotional challenges, their therapy may need to evolve to address these new areas. For instance, the techniques that once helped them feel calm and grounded might need to be adapted to help them manage the more nuanced emotional experiences of adolescence, such as anxiety about peer relationships or navigating a more demanding school environment.

Parents, too, must adapt alongside their children. As a child's needs evolve, so does the role of the parent in supporting therapy. What this means practically is that parents might need to learn new techniques themselves, becoming more attuned to how their child's developmental stage influences their reactions to certain exercises or situations. For example, the comforting touch or simple movement exercises that worked when the child was younger might need to give way to more structured activities that challenge their growing sense of independence.

In many cases, it's also important to revisit the types of sensory experiences the child is exposed to. As children grow, they may become more tolerant of certain sensory inputs, or they may develop new sensitivities. Parents can work closely with therapists to fine-tune the types of activities that help their child feel comfortable and engaged. Maybe a child who once couldn't tolerate being touched can now handle certain types of tactile input. Or perhaps they've developed a greater need for proprioceptive feedback—movements that help them feel where their body is in space—and therapy must adapt to provide more opportunities for deep pressure or resistance activities.

Ultimately, the key to adapting and evolving somatic therapy is staying responsive to the child's changing needs and strengths. Progress in therapy is not always predictable or linear, and that's okay. The real magic happens when parents and therapists come together to create a flexible, dynamic approach that honors where the child is right now while gently nudging them toward continued growth.

This evolving process requires patience and creativity, but it also brings about a deeper understanding of the child as an individual—one whose needs will continue to shift as they move through the different stages of life. For parents, this journey can be both rewarding and challenging, but by remaining open to change and committed to working in partnership with their child's therapist, they can ensure that the therapy continues to offer meaningful support as their child grows.

Chapter 10

What the Future Holds for Your Child

Somatic therapy can be a transformative tool in laying the foundation for a child's long-term success, particularly in building emotional resilience, improving motor skills, and enhancing overall well-being. What makes somatic therapy so powerful is its gentle, body-centered approach that acknowledges the intricate relationship between the body, emotions, and mind. For children on the autism spectrum, who often struggle with sensory processing, anxiety, and emotional regulation, this approach offers a way to connect with their internal experiences in a more grounded and manageable way.

At its core, somatic therapy teaches children to become aware of their bodies and how they react to the world around them. This awareness is key to developing emotional resilience, a skill that will serve them not just in childhood but throughout their lives. Children with autism can often feel overwhelmed by their emotions, especially when they are overstimulated or anxious. Through somatic therapy, they learn to recognize the physical sensations that come with stress—tight muscles, shallow breathing, or a racing heart—and respond to them in a calming, intentional way. By teaching children how to pause, breathe deeply, and release tension, somatic therapy gives them practical tools to self-regulate when emotions run high. This kind of body awareness builds the resilience they need to navigate challenging situations without becoming overwhelmed.

Over time, this consistent practice of tuning into their bodies helps children internalize these coping mechanisms, enabling them to respond to stress with greater ease. The beauty of somatic therapy is that it respects each child's pace—there's no rush or pressure to perform. Instead, the emphasis is on small, consistent steps that accumulate over time, resulting in long-lasting emotional strength. As children grow, this foundation of emotional resilience helps them face life's inevitable challenges with greater confidence and calm, knowing they have tools within themselves to find balance when they need it.

In addition to emotional resilience, somatic therapy has a profound impact on motor skills. Many children with autism struggle with motor coordination, whether it's fine motor tasks like holding a pencil or gross motor skills like running or jumping. Somatic therapy works by helping children feel more in tune with their physical movements, which in turn improves their ability to control and coordinate their bodies. Through slow, mindful movements and exercises designed to engage different muscle groups, children learn to strengthen their motor pathways in a way that feels safe and comfortable. Over time, these exercises help improve muscle tone, balance, and coordination, making everyday tasks easier to manage.

For example, something as simple as learning to shift weight from one foot to another during a somatic exercise can enhance balance, while gentle stretching can increase flexibility and body control. These small, achievable gains build upon each other, eventually translating into improved motor function. What's especially important to note is that these exercises don't just focus on the body in isolation— they also encourage emotional and sensory integration. When children can move more freely and confidently, they often experience a reduction in anxiety and an increase in their overall sense of well-being. The body and mind work together, and the progress made in one area naturally supports the other.

Somatic therapy's impact on overall well-being goes beyond emotional and physical gains—it also fosters a sense of inner peace and calm that many children with autism find elusive. By learning to slow down, breathe deeply, and listen to their bodies, children develop a deeper connection to themselves, which can dramatically reduce feelings of sensory overload and anxiety. This newfound sense of calm can be life-changing, particularly for children who have spent much of their lives feeling disconnected from their own bodies or overwhelmed by their environment. With consistent practice, children can achieve a more grounded and centered state of being, one that allows them to experience the world with less fear and more openness.

The key to success with somatic therapy, as with any therapeutic approach, is consistency and patience. Results do not happen overnight, and it's important to approach each session with a spirit of openness and trust in the process. Children need time to integrate these new skills, and progress can sometimes be slow or uneven. However, with steady practice and gentle encouragement, the small victories start to add up. It's often in these quiet moments of practice where the most significant growth occurs—when a child starts to recognize how they can calm themselves during a stressful moment or when they master a physical movement that once seemed impossible. Over time, these cumulative gains become a strong foundation for lasting success.

Consistency also builds a sense of safety for the child. When they know what to expect, whether it's a weekly session with a therapist or a daily moment of mindful movement with a caregiver, it helps to reduce anxiety and create a rhythm that supports ongoing growth. Patience is equally important—not just from the child but from the adults who support them. There will be moments of frustration, setbacks, and challenges along the way. However, it's in these moments that the most profound shifts often happen. By remaining patient and compassionate, we create a supportive space where children feel empowered to keep trying, to keep exploring, and to keep growing at their own pace.

Somatic therapy is a gift that continues to give long after the therapy sessions are over. The emotional resilience, improved motor skills, and enhanced well-being that children gain through this work lay a foundation that will support them well into their future. Whether it's handling the stress of a new environment, participating more confidently in social settings, or simply feeling more at ease in their own bodies, the skills learned through somatic therapy will continue to enrich their lives for years to come.

Moving From Childhood to Adolescence

As your child transitions from childhood into adolescence, it's natural to feel a mix of anticipation and uncertainty. This period is marked by profound changes—emotionally, physically, and socially—and for children with autism, these shifts can feel particularly overwhelming. As a parent, one of the most important things you can do is to maintain a sense of steadiness, even as everything around your child seems to be in flux. Continuing to incorporate somatic therapy into their routine can be a powerful way to support them through this transitional phase, helping them stay grounded while navigating the complexities of adolescence.

During adolescence, sensory sensitivities often intensify. The body changes rapidly during puberty, and the emotional upheavals that come with it can leave your child feeling more disoriented and disconnected than usual. Somatic therapy offers a way to anchor them amidst these turbulent shifts. By focusing on body awareness and calming the nervous system, you're giving your child a toolkit to manage feelings of overstimulation or anxiety. For example, gentle breathwork or simple grounding exercises can help your child return to a place of calm when they're feeling overwhelmed. As their body grows, and as their emotional landscape becomes more complex, these familiar somatic practices can serve as a comforting constant.

It's also important to acknowledge that adolescence is a time when social pressures mount. Navigating friendships, dealing with peer expectations, and experiencing the desire for greater independence can be particularly challenging for children on the spectrum. Somatic therapy can help with this, too. By encouraging your child to remain in touch with their body, you're helping them cultivate self-awareness. This awareness can empower them to recognize when they're becoming overwhelmed in social situations or feeling anxious about changes in their peer relationships. It's about giving them the tools to self-regulate, so they can engage with the world on their terms, without feeling trapped by the pressures around them.

Another significant aspect of adolescence is the search for identity. During this stage, children often become more aware of how they are perceived by others, and for a child with autism, this awareness can bring about feelings of isolation or frustration. Somatic therapy can help your child develop a stronger sense of self by teaching them to feel more at home in their own body. When children feel grounded physically, they are more likely to develop confidence in who they are, regardless of external judgments. By continuing the body-based practices of somatic therapy, you are helping your child build an internal sense of safety and identity that can carry them through the uncertainties of adolescence.

As your child grows, you might also notice that their emotional responses become more intense. Mood swings, feelings of insecurity, and heightened anxiety are common in adolescence, and for children with autism, these emotional peaks can be more difficult to manage. Somatic therapy's emphasis on regulating the nervous system can be particularly helpful here. Teaching your child to recognize early signs of emotional overwhelm and guiding them through calming techniques—whether it's deep breathing, sensory integration exercises, or grounding movements—can give them the ability to self-soothe during these difficult moments.

Another challenge that often emerges during adolescence is the struggle for independence. Your child may want to assert more control over their daily routines and decisions, but may also feel conflicted about how to handle this new responsibility. As parents, it can be difficult to find the right balance between offering support and encouraging independence. Somatic therapy can play a key role in this process by fostering a sense of autonomy.

When your child learns to tune into their body's needs and responses, they are developing the capacity to take ownership of their self-care. This doesn't mean withdrawing your support, but rather, giving your child the space to begin making choices about how they engage with somatic practices. Whether it's choosing a particular exercise they find calming or knowing when they need a break, somatic therapy can help them develop a sense of control over their body and their environment.

As you continue to integrate somatic practices into your child's life, remember that the practices themselves may need to evolve as your child grows. What worked when they were younger may need to be adapted to suit their changing needs and preferences. Adolescents are often more self-conscious about their bodies, and some exercises may feel more awkward or less engaging as they become more aware of their physical appearance. The key is to remain flexible, offering new ways to practice somatic therapy that feel appropriate for their age. You might shift toward exercises that offer more privacy or introduce techniques that feel more age-appropriate, such as mindful movement or yoga-inspired practices that cater to a growing adolescent's sense of individuality.

Through it all, what remains constant is the importance of fostering a compassionate and non-judgmental environment. Adolescence is a time when children often experience heightened emotions, and they need to know that they have a safe space to explore these feelings. Somatic therapy offers not just physical tools, but also a philosophy of self-acceptance. By continuing to model patience and understanding, you're showing your child that it's okay to feel out of control sometimes, and that there are ways to navigate these feelings without shame or fear. This message becomes even more important during the teenage years when the pressures to conform or fit in can be overwhelming.

As your child transitions into adolescence, the path may feel uncertain, but the practices and principles of somatic therapy provide a solid foundation on which to build. By helping your child stay connected to their body, you are equipping them with lifelong tools that will support them through not only this transition, but many others to come. Together, you can face the challenges of adolescence with confidence, knowing that there are ways to foster calm, resilience, and growth, no matter what changes lie ahead.

Encouraging Independence and Self-Regulation as Your Child Grows

Somatic therapy offers a powerful pathway for children with autism to develop independence and self-regulation skills in ways that may feel more natural and less forced than traditional therapeutic methods. By focusing on the body and its connection to the mind, somatic therapy helps children become more aware of their physical sensations, movements, and the ways these elements are linked to their emotions and behaviors. Over time, this heightened awareness becomes a tool that children can use to calm themselves, reduce anxiety, and navigate daily routines with greater confidence.

At its core, somatic therapy encourages children with autism to tune into their bodies and recognize the cues that signal when they're feeling overwhelmed, stressed, or dysregulated. For many children on the spectrum, verbalizing emotions or recognizing when they're becoming overstimulated can be challenging. However, somatic therapy bypasses the need for language by inviting children to experience what's happening in their bodies. They might notice the tightening of muscles, the quickening of their heartbeat, or the feeling of tension rising in their shoulders. Once they become attuned to these sensations, they can begin to take small steps toward regulating their responses—whether by practicing calming movements, deep breathing, or other techniques that they've learned in therapy.

As children gain more control over these responses, their ability to self-regulate increases, which naturally leads to greater independence. Imagine a child who, in the past, would have struggled with transitions or overwhelming sensory environments. Through somatic therapy, this child may learn to recognize the early signs of overstimulation and take action before it escalates. Maybe they'll practice a grounding exercise they've learned, or take a moment to focus on their breath, slowing everything down before it becomes too much. These are the building blocks of self-regulation—simple, mindful actions that allow children to remain in control of their bodies and their emotions.

As children begin to master these skills, parents can help them take even more ownership of their therapy and daily routines. Encouraging your child to apply what they've learned in therapy to their everyday life is one of the most empowering things you can do. Instead of framing somatic therapy as something that only happens in a structured, therapeutic setting, parents can weave it into the fabric of daily life. For example, you might gently remind your child to check in with their body during moments of stress or invite them to lead a short somatic exercise before bed or during times of transition, like before school or after a long day.

As your child matures, giving them more autonomy in their therapy can also make a huge difference. It's important to offer choices rather than directives—letting your child pick which somatic exercises feel best to them or when they want to practice them. This creates a sense of ownership over their therapy, rather than making it feel like another obligation or chore. When children feel like active participants in their healing, they are more likely to engage with the process and to use the tools they've learned independently.

Daily routines can also become opportunities for your child to exercise their self-regulation skills. As your child grows, encourage them to take on small responsibilities related to their body awareness. For instance, you could work together to create a morning routine that incorporates body-based practices like gentle stretching or sensory-based exercises that help them feel more centered before starting their day. Over time, you can slowly transition more of these responsibilities to your child, allowing them to decide when and how to incorporate these strategies into their routine.

It's also important to foster a sense of flexibility and curiosity around somatic therapy. Rather than pressuring your child to follow a strict regimen, offer the space for exploration. Some days, they might not want to do a particular exercise, and that's okay. The key is to create an environment where somatic awareness becomes second nature, something your child can draw on whenever they need it, without feeling confined by rigid expectations.

Parents can also model these practices themselves. When children see their parents using body-based strategies to regulate their own stress or maintain balance in their daily lives, they're more likely to adopt these behaviors as well. It sends a powerful message: self-regulation and independence are lifelong skills, and they can be nurtured and refined at any stage.

Somatic therapy offers children with autism a unique and empowering way to connect with their bodies and develop skills that will serve them well into adulthood. With time, patience, and gentle encouragement, parents can help their children build the foundations of independence—both in how they manage their emotions and how they navigate the world around them. It's about providing the tools, the space, and the support for your child to take ownership of their own growth, one mindful step at a time.

Continuing to Support Your Child's Emotional and Physical Well-Being

As you embark on this journey with your child, it's important to remember that somatic therapy is not a quick fix or a one-time solution—it's an ongoing process of growth and discovery. Just as your child continues to develop and change, so too will their needs and the ways in which they respond to somatic practices. This is why viewing somatic therapy as a journey, rather than a destination, is so crucial. It's a journey that requires patience, openness, and most of all, the unwavering support of a loving parent like you.

One of the most powerful aspects of somatic therapy is that it evolves alongside your child. What works for them today may shift as they grow older, as they encounter new challenges, and as their body and mind continue to develop. And that's perfectly okay. Rather than seeking a fixed outcome, the goal is to nurture a deep connection between your child and their body—a connection that will serve them throughout their life. Somatic therapy provides them with tools they can carry forward, tools that will help them self-regulate, find calm in moments of stress, and experience their body as a source of strength and comfort.

As a parent, your role in this journey is invaluable. You are your child's greatest advocate and cheerleader, and your involvement makes a world of difference. The way you engage with your child during somatic therapy—your willingness to explore these practices together, your encouragement when they encounter difficulties, and your celebration of their progress, no matter how small—creates a supportive environment in which they can thrive. It's your presence and belief in them that fuels their confidence, helping them to feel safe and secure as they navigate the challenges of their unique sensory world.

There will be days when somatic practices feel effortless and transformative, and there will be days when they feel slow or frustrating. In those moments of challenge, it's important to remember that growth often happens in the quiet spaces between visible progress. Just as a tree doesn't grow overnight, but strengthens its roots little by little, so too does your child's relationship with their body deepen over time. Somatic therapy is about planting seeds—seeds that may take time to sprout, but once they do, can grow into something lasting and profound.

The benefits of this work extend far beyond the immediate present. As your child grows into adulthood, the foundation you're building today will continue to support them. The ability to tune into their body, to recognize and soothe their own nervous system, and to move through the world with greater ease—these are gifts that will accompany them throughout their life. Whether they're facing the pressures of school, navigating friendships, or adjusting to the demands of work and independence, the body-based awareness cultivated through somatic therapy will serve as a wellspring of resilience and balance.

So, keep going. Keep showing up for your child, even on the days when the progress feels slow or uncertain. This journey is not linear, but every step forward—no matter how small—is meaningful. You're not just helping your child today; you're empowering them with lifelong skills that will allow them to face the world with confidence, self-awareness, and calm. There's no rush, no perfect path—just the steady unfolding of growth and connection that comes with time, love, and patience.

As you continue to walk this path together, remind yourself of the incredible power of simply being present. Your love, your dedication, and your commitment to this journey are the most important gifts you can offer your child.

Part 7: Long-Term Benefits of Somatic Therapy for Children with Autism

Chapter 11

Empowering Your Child for the Future

Somatic therapy is more than just a short-term intervention; it's a pathway that equips children with autism with skills they can carry with them throughout their lives. By focusing on the body as a gateway to emotional and physical well-being, somatic therapy provides children with practical tools for self-regulation, motor coordination, and, perhaps most importantly, confidence. These tools don't just help children manage the challenges they face in the present, but also set the stage for their long-term success, empowering them as they move through adolescence into adulthood.

One of the key areas where somatic therapy shines is in emotional regulation. For children on the autism spectrum, managing emotions can often feel like an overwhelming task, especially in situations that involve sensory overload or unexpected changes in routine. Somatic therapy addresses this by teaching children to reconnect with their bodies in ways that calm the nervous system and create a sense of safety. When a child learns to focus on their breath, feel the weight of their body on the ground, or gently engage in repetitive, rhythmic movements, they're not just calming down in the moment—they're building the skills to navigate emotional ups and downs more effectively in the future. Over time, these body-based practices become second nature, offering a sense of control that is both empowering and grounding.

For example, a child who has practiced somatic breathing exercises during therapy may, over time, begin to use those same techniques in real-world situations, such as before a stressful school presentation or in a crowded, noisy environment. Instead of feeling helpless in the face of anxiety, they have tools at their disposal—tools that don't require external intervention, but instead come from within their own body. This is the beauty of somatic therapy: it fosters self-reliance. Children learn that they can tune into their body's signals and take proactive steps to calm themselves down, rather than feeling at the mercy of their emotions.

In addition to emotional regulation, somatic therapy has a profound impact on motor skills, which are often areas of difficulty for children with autism. Many children on the spectrum struggle with coordination, balance, and fine motor control, which can affect everything from playing with peers to performing basic daily tasks. Somatic therapy works on these issues in a gentle, integrative way. Through movements that emphasize body awareness, children gradually improve their balance, flexibility, and strength. These exercises are not about achieving perfection but about fostering a better relationship between the mind and body. As children learn to move with greater ease and precision, they begin to experience a sense of physical competence that translates into other areas of life.

Improved motor skills also play a crucial role in boosting a child's confidence. For many children with autism, difficulty with physical tasks can lead to frustration and feelings of inadequacy. However, when they begin to experience small victories—such as catching a ball, successfully walking along a balance beam, or even sitting with good posture—it builds a quiet confidence within them. These seemingly simple achievements have a ripple effect: they make children more willing to engage with their environment, participate in group activities, and try new things. With each step forward, children start to see themselves as capable, and that sense of capability is a cornerstone for long-term success.

Confidence, perhaps more than anything, is what somatic therapy nurtures over time. It's not the kind of confidence that comes from external praise or accomplishments, but the kind that comes from feeling secure in one's own body and abilities. As children on the spectrum develop these skills, they start to trust themselves more. They understand that, even in the face of challenges, they have the ability to regulate their emotions, control their movements, and adapt to new situations. This inner confidence allows them to take risks, explore their interests, and pursue goals they might have otherwise avoided out of fear or uncertainty.

Moreover, the benefits of somatic therapy extend beyond the individual child. As they gain emotional regulation, improved motor skills, and confidence, they become more engaged with the world around them. This can enhance their social relationships, make school environments more accessible, and help them build stronger connections with peers and caregivers. Over time, these foundational skills help children integrate more smoothly into the wider community, setting them up for success not only in childhood but also as they transition into adulthood.

In this way, somatic therapy serves as a powerful tool for long-term success. It doesn't promise instant results or a one-size-fits-all solution, but it does offer a steady, nurturing path that builds resilience, independence, and well-being from the inside out. Through body-based practices, children learn to anchor themselves in moments of stress, to feel empowered by their growing physical abilities, and to approach life with a sense of calm confidence. These are skills that will serve them well as they navigate the future, giving them a solid foundation to face whatever challenges lie ahead.

Encouraging Independence Through Somatic Practices

Somatic therapy has the unique ability to help children with autism develop a sense of independence by deepening their connection with their own bodies. For many children on the spectrum, their bodies can often feel like foreign or unpredictable territory. Sensory overload, anxiety, and difficulty processing physical sensations can make it challenging for them to feel in control of their own emotional and physical responses. Somatic therapy steps in by offering children a gentle, non-invasive way to explore and understand these sensations, gradually helping them build the skills needed for self-regulation and, ultimately, independence.

At its core, somatic therapy is about fostering self-awareness. Through a series of body-based exercises, children learn to pay attention to what their bodies are communicating. This can be as simple as recognizing when their muscles are tense or when their heart is racing. By developing this awareness, children begin to understand the cues their bodies give them before they become overwhelmed. For example, a child who learns to notice the early signs of anxiety—perhaps a tightening in the chest or a feeling of restlessness—can then take steps to manage that emotion before it spirals into a full-blown meltdown.

Somatic exercises also teach children to differentiate between different emotional and physical states. Many children with autism struggle with interoception—the ability to sense and interpret internal bodily signals. A child may not be able to recognize when they are hungry, tired, or even in pain, leading to frustration and behavioral challenges. Somatic therapy works to bridge this gap by helping children practice tuning into these signals. Over time, children become more adept at interpreting what their bodies are trying to tell them, which is a fundamental step toward independence. Imagine a child who, after working through somatic exercises, can identify that they are feeling anxious before a social situation. Armed with that knowledge, they can then use self-soothing techniques they've learned through therapy, such as deep breathing or slow, grounding movements, to calm themselves without needing external intervention.

One of the greatest benefits of somatic therapy is that it equips children with practical tools they can use in everyday life. These exercises are not just confined to the therapy room; they can be incorporated into daily routines, giving children the opportunity to practice self-regulation in real-world settings. For instance, a child who struggles with sensory overload in noisy environments might use a somatic grounding technique, like pressing their feet firmly into the ground or placing a hand on their chest, to center themselves and reduce feelings of overwhelm. The beauty of these techniques is that they are simple, unobtrusive, and can be done anywhere, offering children the autonomy to manage their responses without drawing attention to themselves.

Somatic therapy also promotes self-care, which is another cornerstone of independence. When children learn to listen to their bodies, they become more capable of making choices that support their well-being. This might include recognizing when they need a break, choosing activities that help them feel calm, or even developing routines that prioritize relaxation and sensory comfort. For example, a child who has developed an understanding of how certain environments affect their sensory processing might learn to advocate for themselves by asking for quiet time or using noise-canceling headphones. In this way, somatic therapy not only teaches children to care for themselves but also empowers them to communicate their needs to others—an essential life skill for building independence.

Additionally, somatic exercises often involve movements that help children improve their motor coordination, which can translate into increased physical independence. Many children with autism experience challenges with motor planning, making it difficult for them to complete everyday tasks like dressing themselves, using utensils, or participating in physical activities. Through repetitive, mindful movement practices, somatic therapy helps strengthen the neural pathways that support motor skills, enabling children to become more confident in their ability to navigate their physical environment. As they gain mastery over their own movements, children experience a sense of achievement and control, which fosters a deeper sense of independence.

Moreover, somatic therapy teaches children how to cope with the physical manifestations of stress, which is critical for developing emotional resilience. By learning how to manage their physiological responses to stress—whether it's through breathing exercises, gentle stretches, or grounding techniques—children gain the capacity to calm themselves in challenging situations. This self-regulation is the key to fostering independence because it reduces their reliance on external support when they face emotional difficulties. Over time, children come to understand that they have the tools within themselves to manage discomfort, which not only enhances their self-confidence but also encourages them to take on new challenges, knowing they can handle the emotional ups and downs that may arise.

In a broader sense, somatic therapy helps children with autism build the foundation for independence by teaching them to trust their own bodies. For many on the spectrum, the body can feel like an unpredictable or even overwhelming space. Somatic therapy helps to shift that narrative, creating a safe and predictable relationship with the body. As children begin to trust that they can influence their own physical and emotional states through movement and self-awareness, they develop a sense of agency over their own lives. This sense of agency is crucial for independence because it encourages children to take initiative, make decisions, and feel confident in their ability to care for themselves as they grow older.

Ultimately, somatic therapy empowers children with autism by giving them the tools and confidence to navigate both their internal world and the external environment. It fosters self-awareness, emotional regulation, physical independence, and self-care, all of which are essential for leading a more independent and fulfilling life. Through this body-based approach, children can learn to recognize their own needs, manage their emotions, and take steps toward becoming more self-sufficient.

Supporting Your Child's Continued Growth Beyond Therapy Sessions

Once formal somatic therapy sessions have ended, the journey of supporting your child's growth doesn't stop. In fact, this is where the real, day-to-day magic happens. As a parent, you have the incredible opportunity to weave the principles of somatic therapy into the very fabric of your child's daily life. By doing this, you create a space where ongoing benefits can flourish and where your child can continue to grow, feel supported, and gain confidence in their body and their ability to navigate the world. The key is consistency, but not rigidity. Somatic principles can be introduced into routines in a way that feels natural, almost seamless, ensuring that your child continues to build on the foundation established during therapy.

One of the most effective ways to carry forward the essence of somatic therapy is through mindful movement. Whether it's during morning stretches, while transitioning from one activity to another, or even in moments of play, encouraging your child to stay connected to their body through simple, intentional movements can help them remain grounded. Gentle stretches that elongate the muscles, slow, rhythmic movements that engage the joints, or even playful activities like balancing games can all promote body awareness. These don't have to be lengthy or structured. In fact, the beauty of somatic work lies in its adaptability. A few moments of focused movement here and there throughout the day can do wonders for maintaining the benefits your child experienced during therapy.

Another important aspect is helping your child tune into their internal sensations, something we call "interoception" in somatic therapy. This can be as simple as asking, "How does your body feel right now?" or encouraging them to notice when they're feeling tightness, warmth, or calm in different parts of their body. For children on the autism spectrum, who may often struggle with understanding their own physical and emotional cues, this practice is invaluable. By bringing their attention to their bodily sensations, you're giving them the tools to recognize when they're beginning to feel overwhelmed or overstimulated, and more importantly, you're showing them that it's okay to pause, take a breath, and attend to their needs.

Breathing exercises are another powerful tool that parents can easily incorporate into daily life. Deep, diaphragmatic breathing helps calm the nervous system and can be especially helpful during transitions or stressful moments. Encouraging your child to take a few deep breaths before heading into a new environment, or when they feel anxious, can help them self-regulate. You can turn this into a shared practice, modeling deep breathing yourself and making it a calm, bonding moment. Over time, your child will come to understand that they can rely on their breath as a source of stability whenever they need it, whether you're there to guide them or not.

Rituals and routines also play a big part in helping your child feel safe and grounded. By incorporating somatic principles into daily routines—whether it's during mealtimes, bedtime, or even while getting ready for school—you help create a predictable rhythm that fosters a sense of security. This could be as simple as giving them a few moments to engage in a grounding exercise before bed, or taking a few minutes at the start of the day to stretch and breathe together. Consistent rituals offer a safe container for their growth and self-exploration, while also reinforcing the somatic tools they've learned in therapy.

Nature can also be a powerful ally in continuing somatic work. Time spent outdoors, moving through natural environments, offers a rich sensory experience that engages the body in a gentle, organic way. Whether it's walking barefoot on grass, feeling the wind on their skin, or listening to the sounds of birds, these experiences can heighten your child's connection to their senses and the world around them. Being in nature naturally encourages somatic awareness—there's something about the simplicity and rhythm of the natural world that invites calm and self-regulation. Regular outings to a park, a nature reserve, or even your backyard can become a cherished part of your routine, offering a way for your child to stay connected to their body while simultaneously feeling the soothing effects of the natural world.

At the core of all these strategies is the idea of making somatic principles part of your everyday life, not as an extra "to-do," but as a way of being with your child. It's about fostering an environment where tuning into the body, moving with awareness, and breathing deeply becomes second nature for both of you. The more you integrate these practices into everyday activities, the more they'll become a natural part of your child's experience. And over time, your child will develop the ability to use these tools independently, gaining a greater sense of autonomy and confidence.

Empowering your child through somatic principles doesn't mean doing everything for them; rather, it's about guiding them to discover their own strength and capacity for self-regulation. This ongoing support requires patience and a gentle touch. Your role is not to push but to offer subtle, consistent encouragement, reminding your child that they have the tools within themselves to feel grounded, calm, and connected.

By continuing to weave these somatic principles into your family's daily life, you're setting the stage for lasting growth. Your child's body will continue to remember and build upon the lessons of therapy, and over time, you'll witness the subtle but profound shifts that come from living a life more connected to the body's wisdom. Your child may still face challenges, but with your ongoing support and the tools of somatic therapy, they'll have a stronger foundation to meet those challenges with resilience and grace.

The Lifelong Benefits of Somatic Therapy

Incorporating somatic therapy into the lives of children with autism can have a profound, lasting impact that extends far beyond childhood. The benefits of these body-based practices ripple through time, providing tools that can enhance their mental, emotional, and physical well-being as they grow into adults. Somatic therapy is not just about managing the challenges children face in the present moment;

it's about equipping them with lifelong skills that will support their ability to navigate a complex world with greater confidence, self-awareness, and resilience.

One of the most significant advantages of somatic therapy is the way it fosters a deep connection between body and mind. For children with autism, sensory overload and difficulty processing physical sensations can lead to heightened anxiety and frustration. Somatic therapy helps them become more attuned to their bodies, teaching them to recognize and interpret physical signals that may have previously been overwhelming or confusing. As they grow older, this awareness becomes a powerful tool for managing stress, anxiety, and emotional dysregulation. Instead of feeling trapped by the sensations their bodies are experiencing, they learn to tune in, breathe through discomfort, and respond with calm instead of panic. This foundational skill allows them to approach challenges—whether academic, social, or professional—with a greater sense of ease and self-regulation.

As these children move into adolescence and adulthood, the physical benefits of somatic therapy continue to unfold. The exercises they practiced as children to improve motor coordination and balance evolve into more sophisticated tools for maintaining overall physical health. Many individuals with autism struggle with motor planning or proprioception—the sense of where their bodies are in space. These challenges don't disappear with age, but the techniques learned through somatic therapy help to minimize their impact over time. As adults, they can carry these practices into their daily lives, using movement-based routines to stay grounded, reduce physical tension, and maintain balance in a way that feels intuitive. Whether it's through yoga, tai chi, or mindful movement exercises, these practices can become lifelong habits that promote physical health, flexibility, and mobility, even as they age.

The emotional resilience developed through somatic therapy also plays a key role in adulthood. Life is full of unpredictable situations, and for individuals on the autism spectrum, navigating social dynamics, career responsibilities, and personal relationships can be particularly challenging. Somatic therapy equips them with tools to handle emotional stress in a healthy, body-centered way. Instead of feeling overwhelmed by anxiety or shutting down in response to sensory overload, they can lean on the grounding exercises they've practiced throughout their lives. Learning to calm the nervous system through breathwork, mindful body awareness, or gentle movement can make the difference between feeling overwhelmed by a stressful situation and being able to approach it with clarity and composure.

Social interaction is another area where somatic therapy can provide lifelong support. Many children with autism experience difficulty interpreting social cues or managing interpersonal relationships. By tuning into their own physical sensations and emotions, somatic therapy helps individuals build a stronger sense of empathy and connection. As they grow older, the ability to read their own body's signals can translate into greater social awareness. They become better equipped to understand nonverbal communication, regulate their emotional responses, and engage more meaningfully with others. This emotional intelligence, developed through a deepened connection to their own bodies, enhances their capacity to form and maintain healthy relationships in adulthood.

Somatic therapy's impact on mental health is another profound benefit that extends into the adult years. The stress-reduction techniques learned in childhood continue to serve as effective tools for managing anxiety, depression, or trauma. Many adults on the autism spectrum experience mental health challenges related to the ongoing pressures of sensory processing, social interaction, and the need for routine. By incorporating somatic practices into their daily lives, they can maintain a stronger mental equilibrium, using the body as a resource for calming the mind and stabilizing their emotions. The body's natural ability to self-regulate, when harnessed through these practices, becomes a protective factor against the overwhelm that can come with life's unpredictability.

As adults, individuals who have practiced somatic therapy often experience a greater sense of self-empowerment. They have learned to trust their bodies and have a deeper understanding of their own needs, preferences, and boundaries. This sense of embodiment—of being fully present in one's own body—can help them make better decisions about their health, well-being, and personal relationships. They are more likely to advocate for themselves, set boundaries, and seek out environments and relationships that support their mental, emotional, and physical health.

Furthermore, the ability to connect with their own bodies allows them to cultivate a greater sense of self-compassion. For many adults on the autism spectrum, self-criticism and feelings of inadequacy can be frequent companions, particularly in a world that often misunderstands or undervalues neurodiversity. Somatic therapy fosters a relationship with the body that is grounded in acceptance and kindness. Instead of viewing their sensory sensitivities or physical differences as limitations, they can appreciate the unique ways their bodies move, feel, and respond to the world. This body-based self-acceptance lays the foundation for a more positive relationship with themselves, which is crucial for overall life satisfaction and well-being.

Incorporating somatic therapy into the lives of children with autism is not just about addressing the immediate challenges they face, but about planting seeds for their future. The benefits they gain in childhood—the ability to regulate emotions, manage sensory input, and connect with their bodies—grow with them as they navigate adolescence and adulthood. These practices provide a sense of stability and control, empowering them to meet the demands of an ever-changing world with resilience and strength. As they grow older, they will continue to draw on these skills, finding in them a source of calm, clarity, and empowerment that supports them through every stage of life.

Chapter 12

Maintaining Progress and Staying Connected

Maintaining the progress a child has made through somatic therapy is an ongoing process that requires both consistency and flexibility. As children grow and develop, their needs change, and the strategies that once worked may need to be adapted. However, the good news is that the foundational work done through somatic therapy provides tools that can be carried forward, helping a child navigate these transitions with greater ease and resilience.

One of the key strategies for maintaining progress is to create a routine that incorporates somatic practices into daily life. Just as we brush our teeth or get dressed each day, these body-based exercises can become a natural part of a child's routine. The goal is to normalize the practice so that it doesn't feel like "therapy" but rather something they do to feel good, to center themselves, and to maintain balance.

Children thrive on routine, and when somatic exercises are woven into the fabric of their day, they become habits that support emotional regulation and physical well-being. This could be as simple as a few minutes of guided breathing in the morning to set a calm tone for the day or a few gentle stretches in the evening to help unwind before bed.

Equally important is the concept of responsiveness. As children move through different stages of development, what they need from somatic therapy will evolve. Younger children might respond to playful, movement-based exercises, while older children may benefit more from mindfulness techniques that allow them to tune into their body in quieter ways. It's essential to remain open to adjusting the practices based on what resonates with the child at different ages. Sometimes this means simplifying exercises, and at other times it means introducing more complexity. By staying attuned to the child's developmental needs and interests, we can keep the work relevant and engaging, making it easier for the child to continue using the skills they've learned.

Another important aspect of maintaining progress is fostering emotional connection through the body. Many children on the autism spectrum experience heightened sensitivity to touch and physical sensation. As a result, their relationship with their own body can sometimes feel overwhelming or disconnected. Somatic therapy helps bridge this gap, teaching children to feel more at home in their bodies. As a caregiver or therapist, it's essential to nurture this connection over time by encouraging the child to continue exploring their physical sensations in a safe, non-judgmental way. This might involve helping the child identify and name their emotions through body awareness or guiding them to notice how their body feels in different emotional states, allowing them to build an internal map that supports emotional regulation.

Incorporating these practices into everyday moments can be incredibly powerful. For example, if a child is feeling anxious or overstimulated, gently guiding them to notice their breath or helping them engage in a grounding exercise can prevent escalation. The more these moments of somatic awareness are integrated into daily life, the more the child will come to rely on them as tools for self-soothing and regulation. Over time, the goal is for the child to develop an intuitive sense of when and how to use these techniques without needing outside prompts.

As children grow older and face new challenges, such as entering adolescence or dealing with the increasing social demands of school, it becomes even more crucial to revisit and reinforce the somatic tools they've learned. These transitional periods can be particularly overwhelming, and it's during these times that somatic practices can serve as an anchor. Encouraging the child to continue exploring movement, breath, and mindfulness can help them manage the heightened emotional and sensory experiences that often accompany developmental transitions. Additionally, these practices can serve as a foundation for building resilience, giving the child a sense of control over their own emotional and physical well-being, even in uncertain times.

Another critical element in maintaining progress is the role of the support system around the child. Parents, caregivers, and therapists play an essential part in creating a supportive environment that reinforces the benefits of somatic therapy. This doesn't mean that the child's progress hinges on constant intervention, but rather that the adults in the child's life continue to model and encourage body-based awareness. It can be as simple as practicing somatic exercises together or offering reminders to check in with the body during moments of stress. When the adults around the child also prioritize somatic awareness, it reinforces the idea that this is a lifelong skill, not something they will outgrow.

Consistency is key, but so is patience. There will be times when the child seems to regress or when they lose interest in certain practices. This is natural and part of the ebb and flow of development. The important thing is to gently guide them back to the practices that have helped them in the past, while also allowing space for new explorations. Somatic therapy is not about perfection or rigid adherence to a set of exercises; it's about providing a toolkit that the child can draw from as they need. As they grow, they will continue to refine these tools and adapt them to new situations, whether it's handling the stress of a school project, navigating social interactions, or simply managing everyday sensory overload.

In the long run, maintaining progress through somatic therapy is about fostering a deep sense of body awareness and emotional resilience. It's about giving the child the confidence to trust their own body and its signals and to use that trust as a compass for navigating the world. As they transition through different stages of development, they'll carry these tools with them, not as a burden, but as a source of strength. And as they continue to grow, these somatic practices will evolve alongside them, remaining a vital part of their journey toward emotional and physical well-being.

Staying Connected with Your Child's Therapist and Support Network

Staying connected with your child's therapist and the other professionals involved in their care is one of the most critical elements in maintaining their progress through somatic therapy. While it may be tempting to feel like you can ease up after seeing initial improvements, the truth is that ongoing collaboration with these experts ensures that your child continues to grow, adapt, and overcome challenges as they arise. It's an ongoing process—one that needs continuous support, feedback, and adjustment.

The relationship you build with your child's therapist should feel like a partnership. You're both working toward the same goal: supporting your child's well-being, helping them regulate their emotions, and guiding them toward a more comfortable experience in their body. This partnership requires open, regular communication. Your child's therapist brings expertise in somatic practices, a deep understanding of body-based approaches, and insight into how autism affects children on many different levels. But you, as the parent, are the expert on your child. You know their daily routines, their emotional triggers, and their responses to different situations. When you stay connected with the therapist, you're providing invaluable context that can help tailor the therapy sessions to meet your child's evolving needs.

There will be times when things don't go as smoothly as hoped—moments when your child's behavior regresses or when they struggle with a new challenge.

These are the moments when staying connected with your child's therapist becomes even more important. Rather than feeling frustrated or discouraged, you can reach out, share what's happening, and collaborate on how to adjust the therapy approach. The therapist may recommend modifications to the somatic exercises, suggest new techniques, or offer insights into why a particular challenge is occurring. Together, you can problem-solve and find solutions that keep your child moving forward, even during difficult times.

Ongoing communication also allows the therapist to track your child's progress in a more meaningful way. Therapy is not a static process; it's dynamic and ever-changing, much like your child. As they grow, their needs will shift, and the therapy should evolve alongside them. Regular check-ins, whether through in-person meetings, phone calls, or even emails, give the therapist a clear picture of how your child is doing outside of the therapeutic environment. This information helps guide future sessions, ensuring that the therapy remains effective and relevant. It also provides you with the opportunity to ask questions, share observations, and feel more confident in your role as an active participant in your child's healing journey.

But it's not just the therapist you need to stay connected with—it's also the broader network of professionals who play a role in your child's care. This might include occupational therapists, speech therapists, educators, or even pediatricians. Each of these professionals brings a unique perspective, and when they work together, they can provide a more holistic approach to your child's development. For instance, an occupational therapist might notice something about your child's motor skills that complements the work being done in somatic therapy. Or a teacher might share insights about how your child is applying calming techniques in the classroom. By staying in communication with these professionals, you create a circle of care around your child, ensuring that everyone is on the same page and working in harmony to support your child's growth.

In many ways, this ongoing collaboration acts as a safety net. It's easy to feel overwhelmed as a parent, especially when you're navigating a complex array of therapies and treatments. Staying connected with your child's care team allows you to share the load. You don't have to have all the answers or carry the entire burden on your own. The professionals involved in your child's care are there to help, to guide, and to offer support when you need it. When you reach out, when you ask questions, and when you keep the lines of communication open, you're strengthening that safety net—ensuring that no detail is overlooked and that your child's progress is consistently monitored.

Finally, staying connected also offers emotional reassurance. It's easy to second-guess yourself as a parent, especially when your child is facing unique challenges. Regular communication with your child's therapist and care team can remind you that you're not alone in this journey. Their expertise and encouragement can help you feel more grounded, more confident in your parenting, and more hopeful about your child's future. You'll also find that they can help you celebrate the small victories—the little moments of progress that might otherwise go unnoticed. These professionals can offer perspective, reminding you that even the smallest shifts in your child's behavior or body awareness are worth celebrating.

In essence, maintaining an ongoing connection with your child's therapist and other professionals is about creating a consistent support system. It ensures that your child's progress is nurtured over time and that any challenges are met with a collaborative, informed response. It's a dynamic, evolving partnership that works to bring out the best in your child and offers you the peace of mind that you are doing everything possible to support their development in a way that is both compassionate and effective.

Building a Supportive Community for Your Child's Ongoing Growth

Building a supportive community around a child with autism is one of the most important steps parents can take to ensure lasting progress and emotional well-being. While somatic therapy offers powerful tools to help children connect with their bodies, manage anxiety, and improve motor skills, it works best when woven into a larger network of understanding and care. This is where the community—made up of family, friends, therapists, educators, and others who interact with your child—comes into play. Creating a circle of support around your child can provide not only practical help but also emotional reinforcement for both you and your child as you navigate the ups and downs of their development.

At the heart of this process is the need for clear, open communication. As a parent, you are your child's biggest advocate, and your ability to communicate their needs, challenges, and progress to others is crucial. Start by involving those closest to your child—family members and friends—who interact with them regularly. It's important to take time to explain what somatic therapy is, how it works, and why it's beneficial for your child. Since somatic therapy might not be familiar to everyone, offering simple, relatable examples can help bridge the gap. You could describe how body-based techniques help your child self-regulate when they're feeling overwhelmed or how certain movements calm their nervous system and foster a sense of security. When those around your child understand the goals and the mechanisms of somatic therapy, they're better equipped to offer meaningful support.

In many cases, family and friends may have their own expectations or ideas about how to help your child, which may not always align with the practices of somatic therapy. This is where patience and education come in. Encourage them to observe the positive changes they see in your child's behavior, mood, or physical skills after a therapy session or practice. Sometimes, seeing these small victories firsthand helps others appreciate the value of somatic therapy and makes them more likely to embrace it. It's also important to express that somatic therapy is not a quick fix, but a process that requires consistency and support from everyone involved. The more family and friends understand the long-term nature of this approach, the more they can provide encouragement without placing undue pressure on your child or you.

Therapists and educators are also key players in your child's support system. These professionals spend significant time with your child and have a unique role in reinforcing the principles of somatic therapy in different settings. Finding therapists who understand and incorporate somatic therapy into their practice is essential. You want to work with professionals who not only have the technical skills but also the empathy to meet your child where they are. These therapists should be viewed as partners in your child's journey. Regularly check in with them to discuss your child's progress, setbacks, and any adjustments that may need to be made. It's a collaborative process, and maintaining a strong relationship with therapists can make all the difference in sustaining progress over time.

Educators, too, need to be brought into the fold, especially if your child is spending a significant portion of their day at school. Speak with teachers and school administrators about the benefits of somatic therapy and how certain practices might help your child in the classroom. Perhaps there are specific body-based exercises that can be integrated into their day to help them stay calm and focused. Again, communication is key here. Teachers are often juggling the needs of many students, but by providing them with practical tools and insights into your child's unique needs, you can help them create an environment that supports your child's progress. It's also worth exploring whether the school offers or would consider integrating somatic practices or related programs into their curriculum for children with autism. When educators understand and support the therapeutic journey, they can be powerful allies in helping your child feel more confident and secure at school.

Outside of immediate family, friends, and professionals, consider seeking out support groups or communities that are already familiar with somatic therapy or who work with children on the spectrum. These communities can offer a wealth of shared experience, advice, and understanding. Whether through local support networks or online forums, connecting with others who are walking a similar path can provide you with fresh perspectives and a sense of solidarity. It's reassuring to know that you're not alone, and sometimes the best advice comes from someone who's facing the same challenges and can offer empathy born from experience. These groups also serve as spaces where you can share your own successes and challenges, creating a sense of mutual encouragement and learning.

Building this broader community doesn't happen overnight, but it's worth the investment of time and effort. Over time, you'll begin to see how the presence of a well-rounded, supportive network can ease your burden and amplify the benefits of somatic therapy for your child. Whether it's a friend offering to practice gentle somatic movements during a playdate or a teacher incorporating calming techniques into the school day, each small act of understanding contributes to a larger ecosystem of care that surrounds your child.

Ultimately, the goal is to create a circle of support that is flexible, responsive, and grounded in a shared commitment to your child's well-being. Each person in your child's life plays a role, no matter how big or small, in helping them build the skills and resilience they need to thrive. By fostering relationships with those who understand and support somatic therapy practices, you're not just creating a support network— you're building a community where your child can grow, feel understood, and be encouraged to be their authentic self.

A Positive Outlook: Celebrating Your Child's Journey of Growth

As you reflect on the progress your child has made through somatic therapy, it's important to pause and celebrate every milestone, no matter how small it may seem. Each step forward, whether it's a new level of physical coordination, a moment of calm in the midst of sensory overload, or a deepened emotional connection, is a testament to your child's resilience and growth. Somatic therapy is not just about mastering specific skills or exercises—it's about nurturing the whole person, helping your child feel more grounded, more aware, and more at peace with themselves and the world around them. Every breakthrough, no matter how gradual, is a sign that their body and mind are learning to work together in harmony.

This journey is about more than just progress—it's about transformation. You've seen firsthand how tuning into the body can unlock a sense of calm that words alone often can't reach. You've witnessed the subtle shifts in your child's posture, their ability to self-regulate, and their newfound capacity for handling situations that once felt overwhelming. These changes may not always be dramatic, but they are real and profound, laying the foundation for continued growth and well-being. Somatic therapy has offered your child a new way to experience the world—a path to self-discovery that is gentle, supportive, and deeply attuned to their needs.

Along this path, you've been your child's greatest ally. You've shown incredible patience and compassion, allowing the therapy to unfold at your child's pace, never rushing or forcing outcomes. This approach, grounded in understanding and acceptance, has been key to their success. You've embraced the idea that growth is a process, one that sometimes moves slowly but always moves in the right direction when given the right support. And in doing so, you've modeled for your child the power of persistence, the value of self-compassion, and the importance of celebrating every achievement, no matter how small.

As you look ahead, know that this journey will continue to evolve. Somatic therapy has provided a toolkit that your child can carry with them for life, a set of resources that will help them navigate challenges, build resilience, and foster a sense of calm even in the face of difficulty. While the road may still have its ups and downs, the progress your child has made is undeniable—and it's something to take pride in. Every moment of calm they find, every new skill they develop, and every connection they strengthen is a victory worth cherishing.

The beauty of this journey is that it's ongoing, and with each new stage, there will be more opportunities for growth. Your child's body and mind will continue to learn and adapt, and as they do, you'll be there, guiding them with the same love and support that has brought them this far. Remember that there's no final destination—just a continued unfolding of their potential. With every milestone, you're not only helping them grow, but you're also teaching them to embrace their own journey with hope and optimism.

So as you move forward, keep celebrating the progress—both big and small. Embrace the challenges as part of the process, knowing that each one brings new opportunities for learning and growth. And most importantly, hold onto the optimism that has carried you this far. Your child's path may be unique, but it's full of promise, and the foundation you've built together through somatic therapy is one that will continue to support them for years to come.

Conclusion

Your Child's Path to a Calmer, Happier Life

As we reach the end of this journey together, I want to take a moment to reflect on the incredible progress you've made in your child's somatic therapy journey. Think back to where you started, perhaps feeling unsure or overwhelmed by the road ahead. Now, look at the strides you've taken, the small victories, and the profound changes that have unfolded along the way. Every step you've taken, every technique you've tried, and every moment of patience you've shown has contributed to a remarkable transformation, both for you and your child.

Somatic therapy is more than just a set of techniques; it's a pathway to a calmer, happier life for your child. Through this journey, you've not only helped your child connect more deeply with their body and emotions but also empowered yourself to be a more effective, understanding, and supportive caregiver. The hard work you've invested has led to tangible benefits—reduced anxiety, improved motor skills, and a greater sense of calm and connection. These are not just fleeting changes but foundational shifts that can build a brighter future for your child.

Consider the ways somatic therapy has already made a difference. Your child's ability to manage sensory overload, their increased emotional resilience, and their improved physical coordination are testaments to the power of these body-based practices. These improvements don't just impact their daily lives but set the stage for continued growth and development. With each passing day, as you integrate these techniques into your routines, you're nurturing a more balanced, confident, and joyful child.

Yet, the journey doesn't end here. As you finish this book, it's essential to think about the next steps and how to maintain the momentum you've built. Consistency is key. Continue to practice the somatic techniques you've learned, making them a natural part of your child's daily life. The benefits of somatic therapy are most profound when these practices are woven into everyday routines, creating a stable and supportive environment for your child to thrive.

Maintaining regular contact with professionals who understand somatic therapy can also be incredibly beneficial. They can provide ongoing guidance, support, and adjustments to the techniques based on your child's evolving needs. Remember, you don't have to navigate this path alone. The expertise of therapists and support networks can be invaluable in continuing your child's journey toward greater well-being.

Additionally, stay connected with the community of parents, caregivers, and professionals who share your commitment to somatic therapy. Engaging with others who understand the challenges and triumphs can offer a source of encouragement and inspiration. Sharing experiences, insights, and support can help you remain motivated and informed as you move forward.

As you continue to apply these practices and remain dedicated to your child's growth, keep in mind that every challenge you face and every effort you make is contributing to a more harmonious and fulfilling life for your child. Your dedication is making a real difference, and your belief in their potential is a powerful force for positive change.

In closing, I want to leave you with a message of hope and encouragement. The journey you've embarked on may have its ups and downs, but every step forward is a testament to your love and commitment. Believe in the potential for continued growth and happiness that lies ahead. Your child's path to a calmer, happier life is illuminated by your hard work and unwavering support. Embrace the progress you've made, celebrate the victories, and keep moving forward with confidence and hope. The future is bright, and the possibilities are endless.